Praise for *Latinx Business Success*

Frank's book is an excellent roadmap for mentoring and guiding our current and future LatinX leaders across multiple industries in America. Reading about the many Latinx who have played a significant role in the transformation of our nation's advancement in digital technology is inspiring. Frank is a consistent champion of the Latino community, and his book will prove to be both powerful and actionable for those who wish to succeed in our everchanging digital world.

—Jeff Garcia, retired four-time Pro Bowl NFL
Quarterback and business entrepreneur

Frank Carbajal does an outstanding job at gathering invaluable advice from top Latinx leaders across diverse sectors. The stories are compelling and the advice is both powerful and actionable. His DIGITAL leadership model offers practices and strategies to succeed in a digital economy. Highly recommend!

—Dr. Jacinta M. Jiménez, psychologist, technology
executive, and best-selling author of *The Burnout Fix*

Once again Frank Carbajal has proven to be an inspirational writer.

This collection of advice and inspiration is a manual for success through advice from the top industry professionals to examples shown to him by his Latino industry mentors and family.

Frank Carbajal, knocks down the wall of a digital divide and clears the way for your own opportunities in Silicon Valley. Frank boldly shows you how to find your own path to greatness. I only wish it had been written years earlier....

—Rick Najera, award-winning WGA writer and founder of *Latino Thought Makers*, bringing important conversations on culture and race

In *Latinx Business Success: How Latinx Ingenuity, Innovation, and Tenacity are Driving Some of The World's Biggest Companies*, Frank Carbajal and Dr. José Morey have provided an excellent tool to guide and foster Latinx leadership in the business, nonprofit, academic, media, arts, and technology sectors in America. Reading the history and journeys of several amazing Latinx leaders serves as an inspiration to both current leaders and future aspiring leaders. By using the DIGITAL: decision, intelligence, game plan, insight, technology, abundance, and leverage approach to develop leaders, this guide will help to both ensure that the beautiful diversity of our Latinx community is reflected in our American institutions and that such Latinx leadership is effective.

—Laura Farber, immediate past president and Rose Bowl Management Committee chairman 2021–2022

Frank Carbajal has written a must-read for corporate professionals and anyone looking to learn more about the development of digital intelligence. The digital age has ushered in a number of evolutionary phases, and Latinx individuals have been a part of each one. Learn from anecdotes and stories shared by the most prolific leaders in tech, healthcare, academia, media, and more. The DIGITAL framework offers actionable insights for those of us currently navigating the digital economy and shows readers how to effectively continue to make contributions in diverse and ever-expanding sectors. This book is written *about* the best leaders *by* one of the best Latinx leaders out there, Mr. Carbajal.

—Victoria Banuelos, marketing strategist and author,
First-Gen, NextGen

Latinx Business Success: How Latinx Ingenuity, Innovation, and Tenacity are Driving Some of The World's Biggest Companies is not only a book that tells the story of many exceptional Latinxs who have played critical roles in the digital transformation of our nation; it is also an incredibly inspirational story of success and resilience and a dedication to achieving dreams. Despite their very different beginnings, these exceptional leaders have had and continue to have a positive impact in the communities in which they act. These are great leaders that happen to be Latinx.

Frank Carbajal's and Dr. José Morey's idea of deconstructing DIGITAL into seven evolutions is brilliant! It captures the elements of what it takes to become digital and it gives room for the great life stories that make the book so interesting. The journey to digital is one in which we will all be involved; this book is an inspiration to those who are already on it, and those who will join it soon.

I have always admired Frank's dedication to the betterment of the Latino community, and this book adds to my admiration and respect. Dr. José Morey's renowned trajectory as a thought leader and speaker manifests itself in the pages of this book and adds to its message.

—Jorge Titinger, founder and CEO, Titinger Consulting

LATINX BUSINESS SUCCESS

LATINX
BUSINESS
SUCCESS

How Latinx Ingenuity, Innovation, and Tenacity are Driving Some of the World's Biggest Companies

FRANK CARBAJAL / JOSÉ MOREY

FOREWORD BY **SOLOMON D. 'SOL' TRUJILLO**
CHAIRMAN OF TRUJILLO GROUP LLC

WILEY

Published by John Wiley & Sons, Inc., Hoboken, New Jersey.
Published simultaneously in Canada.

For general information on our other products and services or for technical support, please contact our Customer Care Department within the United States at (800) 762-2974, outside the United States at (317) 572-3993 or fax (317) 572-4002.

Wiley publishes in a variety of print and electronic formats and by print-on-demand. Some material included with standard print versions of this book may not be included in e-books or in print-on-demand. If this book refers to media such as a CD or DVD that is not included in the version you purchased, you may download this material at http://booksupport.wiley.com. For more information about Wiley products, visit www.wiley.com.

Library of Congress Cataloging-in-Publication Data

Names: Carbajal, Frank, author. | Morey, José, author.
Title: Latinx business success : how Latinx ingenuity, innovation, and
  tenacity are driving some of the world's biggest companies / Frank
  Carbajal, José Morey.
Description: Hoboken, New Jersey : Wiley, [2022] | Includes index.
Identifiers: LCCN 2021045300 (print) | LCCN 2021045301 (ebook) | ISBN
  9781119840817 (hardback) | ISBN 9781119840831 (adobe pdf) | ISBN
  9781119840800 (epub)
Subjects: LCSH: Hispanic American businesspeople. | Leadership.
Classification: LCC HD2358.5.U6 C38 2022 (print) | LCC HD2358.5.U6
  (ebook) | DDC 658.4/0908968073—dc23
LC record available at https://lccn.loc.gov/2021045300
LC ebook record available at https://lccn.loc.gov/2021045301

Cover Design: Paul McCarthy
Cover Art: Getty Images
    Tape: © Emilija Manevska
    Globe: © Chad Baker

SKY10030304_100121

Dedicate my book to my parents Regino and Hermelinda Carbajal My wife Molly, and children Alia, Myla and Bria

—Frank Carbajal

To my son, José, mis padres, Juan y Ivonne, mi hermano, Juancy, mi hermana, Carmen, mis abeulos, todos mi sobrinos y sobrinas y Puerto Rico. You are always in my heart.

—José Morey

CONTENTS

Contents

FOREWORD

This is an important book at this moment in time as the U.S. Latino population becomes increasingly accountable for the economic well-being of our country. Frank Carbajal learned about economic accountability early in his life while helping his parents make ends meet. His experiences as the son of migrant agricultural workers provides the foundation for this book, which begins with his own story of his journey from a one-bedroom home for his family of seven in El Centro, California, to his successful career in the Silicon Valley.

Carbajal then does the same for many successful Latino and Latina individuals who also came from humble beginnings, faced economic and racist hardships, but found the inner strength to persevere and achieve their dreams. The reader is taken on personal journeys of exemplary leaders in a broad spectrum of sectors of our society.

The author attempts to weave a thread through all of the stories regarding the qualities these role models possess that can be an inspiration to young Latinos and Latinas seeking to find their own way to success. He also calls out his own perspectives, as well as those of his subjects in this book, on what is needed in America to foster the success of this cohort, and to realize the full potential of U.S. Latinos across the country in every sector of our economy.

I believe Frank Carbajal's hope in compiling these inspiring stories is for you, the reader, to find the whole of this book to be greater than the sum of its parts.

—**Sol Trujillo**
Chairman of Trujillo Group LLC

PREFACE

FROM IMPERIAL VALLEY TO THE SILICON VALLEY

My parents' journey started on an adverse path from Mexico to the Imperial Valley of California, in the 1960s during the Bracero Program, which allowed Mexicans to work on their journey toward American citizenship. The youngest of five children, I was born in El Centro, California, on June 19, 1969. My mother shared with me that she worked "like a burro" up until her third trimester, spending 10 to 12 hours a day in the fields. Sometimes she worked in the blistering heat of 110 degrees, often feeling like she wasn't going to make it. Pure determination pushed my mother through these conditions. My father also worked these long hours; however, he was treated with more fairness as a male migrant worker at the time. My parents simply taught us about a good work ethic, but more importantly to take that hard work into the classroom. My father knew how to communicate his thoughts and express his frustration with my mother working these long hours and having to begin work again only a few days after I was born.

My dad at that point began to realize the importance of being a father, a man of the household. We did not have much of a house with seven of us in a one-bedroom home in El Centro, California.

After I was two years old, my father had the ambition to move us to the Santa Clara Valley, today known as the Silicon Valley. In 1973 my parents were fortunate to find positions in canneries, which was an industry that was considered better than working in the fields.

However, my parents could afford to live in only one place: an area known as Meadowfair, which was based in East San José, California, and known as a *barrio* (Spanish-speaking neighborhood).

This was a great success for my father because we moved into a four-bedroom home. Everything my parents needed was within a two-mile radius, such as the well-known Mexican shopping center known as Tropicana, which had everything from clothes to food.

From a bird's-eye view, in the early 1970s the Silicon Valley resembled a salad bowl. About three miles east from my childhood home were orchards for picking seasonal fruit. However, to the west and north of my neighborhood the Silicon Valley companies, such as Apple, were beginning to take shape.

I didn't learn English until the second grade. Being integrated into a mainstream school, I realized at a young age that we were at a disadvantage compared with the kids who were White and Asian and who lived in the middle-class neighborhoods known as Evergreen and Creekside. Many of the White kids were from families of the Mormon faith, and their parents worked in the electronics industry. This neighborhood was about three miles from my neighborhood. They appeared to have everything we did not in terms of connectivity to the school, and the inequity was realized early on. However, what we had in my home was an unconditional love that felt so warm and reassuring. For example, my father was determined to instill confidence in me and protect me from any negative influences.

My working life started when I was eight years old, just about to turn nine.

Every summer, my parents showed my four siblings and me the value of the work ethic by taking us to pick cherries, apricots, and at times strawberries in the Silicon Valley. The most difficult part was waking up between 4:30 and 5:00 a.m. and getting ready to head out for another very long day of manual labor. I remember splashing water on my face to wake up, since I was too young to drink coffee. Without a word of complaint or rebellion, all five of us would pack into our father's 1978 pink Datsun, with silver flames along the side, We didn't bother with seat belts, but I felt safe, because I was with my parents and siblings. This job taught me early on to be respectful of migrant workers, as I was a migrant student. But as a young, curious student I vividly remember gazing out of the side window as we drove to Cupertino to pick some cherries and see some of the neighborhoods surrounding early Silicon Valley companies like Apple, which was based out of the garage of Steve Jobs and Steve Wozniak as they were about to embark on creating a company that would not only change Silicon Valley, but the world.

My early childhood life centered on staying out of trouble, because my father wanted me to keep busy. When I was just 12 years old, in the summers I went with my father to clean offices, a job that he worked part-time for a janitorial company in addition to working full-time at a cannery. I know that my father's intent was to keep me busy on weekends and during the summers, working in the fields to keep me away from some of the kids who had joined a gang in the *barrio*. I believe his motive was to make me realize the significance of an education. He didn't want me to work as hard as he had to; he wanted me to work smarter. During that era in the Silicon Valley the industry was electronics and the product was known as a circuit board, and as first-generation Americans we had never been exposed to this language or concept.

On the weekends when I worked with my father as a janitor, throughout the Silicon Valley and the Venture Capital Mecca of Sand Hill Road, I spent many hours daydreaming. I recall what I was thinking I cleaned the office of the CEO of a successful tortilla company. I was slowly pushing the vacuum cleaner as I admired everything in the office, from the rich smell of mahogany to the awards of recognition he received as an outstanding Latino. I also enjoyed looking at his awards hanging on the wall and the ticket stubs from the first Super Bowl they played in the Silver Dome, which were carefully displayed in a case. My father walked in and interrupted my reverie, shouting "*Hijo*, this is the reason you need to concentrate in school and concentrate on going to college!"

My story, along with those of Dr. José Morey and all great Latino and Latina interviewees, is intended to change the narrative and show how our *Latinx Business Success* will enable a transformation into recruiting more Latinas in leadership positions in corporate America, from C-suite level to boardrooms, from creating a business idea to receiving venture capital funding to executing a business to becoming a successful entrepreneur, in roles ranging from healthcare to technology leaders.

Also, in the areas of media and arts, we show how it is just as important for these industries to have representation in the top Silicon Valley firms in the country.

We also wish to encourage key leadership roles from academia to nonprofits to rising stars, to show Generation Z Latinas and Latinos that anything is possible. To make these roles transparent and accessible we will be sharing the tremendous success stories.

The book also focuses on the evolution of digital Latino intelligence, but to get to these solutions, the stories all have a common thread of the gaps and the digital divide, and explain that the solution is an increasing number of Latino and Latinas participating in the transformation of understanding their significance to technology and how to not only be part of the Silicon Valley and beyond, but to take ownership of the Latino future to follow.

This is our time – Es Tiempo – *it's time to get a piece of that Silicon Valley pie.*

—**Frank Carbajal**
San Francisco, California
September 2021

FROM BORINQUEN TO THE BOARDROOM

I was born in Puerto Rico in the early 1980s and grew up in a *barrio* called El Verde (The Greene) in Caguas. We were a traditional Puerto Rican family. My grandmother was the youngest of nine siblings and had studied nursing; my grandfather spent his entire career as a card dealer at the famous Caribe Hilton in Old San Juan, where he spent 36 years or, as he used to say, "Till the age of Christ," dealing cards to international tourists coming to visit the Island of Enchantment.

My father was an immigrant from the Dominican Republic raised in a small town called Higuey and my mother was a beautiful, strong woman from the island. They met at the University of Puerto Rico and soon started a family. My father finished his studies while my mother both studied and worked from home to tend to the family.

Our family was a typical low- to middle-income family on the island. My grandparents were of more modest means. Although we didn't have all the lavish trappings that others may have had, I never noticed, for we were wealthy in love, in passion, and in aspirations of what life could be.

It was my upbringing in *el barrio* that prepared me for the boardroom today. It was my island upbringing that taught me that family goes beyond the boundaries of blood, and the ideal that the growth and prosperity of community far outweighs that of capital. In short, the things that center me as Hispanic from El Caribe are very much the strengths that I bring to the teams and projects I have had the honor to work alongside.

I remember my grandmother, Amelia Tirado de Lasa, always thinking of others. Despite not having much of her own, she always had much to give. She instilled in us the mentality that if one can eat, then all can eat. I remember her always planning and purchasing potential gifts for people in need even before the person arrived at our home. From my grandfather, Victor Lasa, I learned that it is more important to give than to receive. From an early age we would talk about my future as a physician. Abuelo would always say, *"José por cada dolar que ganes en una clinica, estes seguro que hagas tres clinicas para regalarlo."*

From my father, Juan Manuel Morey, I learned the importance of soft skills. My father always had the amazing gift of understanding a room instantly. Like a live chess game, he could analyze not just the pieces on the board, but what their strengths were and how the game needed to play out for the greatest opportunity of success. His people skills are something I have always admired. I have never met a person that my father could not instinctively read. He was careful to evaluate nuances and interpersonal idiosyncrasies, a skill that served him well throughout his years in management at Honeywell. Dad understood the importance of finding allies in your journey. As the African adage states, "If you want to go fast, go alone, but if you want to go far, go together."

My mother, Carmen Ivonne Morey Lasa, was the heart, soul, and glue of our core family. Like many Hispanic families, our mothers are the foundation on which our life and societies stand. They are our refuge in the storm, strength for the journey ahead, and our ever-present help in times of trouble. My mother was no different. She has been and will always be that and so much more. She was also the person from whom I learned most about creativity and to continually reinvent oneself. Her entrepreneurial pursuits led her to *nunca parar de aprender.* She studied art, linguistics, and design and she always endeavored to pursue her passions. Above all, she held the fierce belief that she, her children, and her children's children could aspire to anything they set their mind on. She never wavered when storms rose and never faltered when the journey seemed arduous.

My mother was always what I call a "no box" type of thinker. She never saw the problem from outside of the box; she would never define it as a box to begin with, for that was too limiting. This is a lesson that I learned well and has brought me from being a child born on the Isle of Enchantment to a leader on Silicon Island. Attention to detail and presentation was another amazing art that my mother taught me over the years. She was very much the embodiment of not dressing for the role you had, but for the role you wish to attain.

Despite the amazing support I have had from strong Hispanic women and men in my life, it has not always been a life of ease. I have most certainly been blessed, of that there is no doubt. But my journey has been wrought with more failures than success, more losses than wins. I have experienced racism in many forms. At times it would be blatant and raw, such as a pejorative slur or racial epithet. Other times it would be more subtle and nefarious, such as being passed over for a leadership role or becoming aware of income inequality. Both have been challenges but the latter is oftentimes more grating, due to the information coming with a smile from someone who was either ignorant to their own bias or too biased to their own ignorance. The sad reality of both experiences, however, is that they don't stop when you leave the barrio and enter the boardroom and, in some instances, they worsen.

Despite many failures and missteps, I have always carried with me the teachings of my youth. Like manna from heaven, they have been an ever-present sustenance in times of wandering. The timeless echoes of my parents and my grandparents' teachings have allowed me to live out the words of Samuel Beckett: "Ever tried. Ever failed. No matter. Try again. Fail again. Fail better." It has been El Barrio that has led me to the boardroom. It has been the lessons from the Island of Enchantment that have led me to Silicon Island, and I truly believe all Latinos can do so as well, together.

For with great hardship comes great opportunity. I believe Latinos from all stripes, creeds, and countries have the potential to unleash an economic and educational renaissance throughout the world unlike any time in human history if we focus on the future – and that future is STEM.

I believe there is not only a need but an opportunity for Latinos to transform themselves into the future powerhouse of STEM jobs by focusing on education at all levels and harnessing the budding tech industry developing across the world.

Systemic inequality has been a barrier to the boardroom for far too many and the tinder of racisms has left many careers smoldering throughout history. But from the ashes of calamity, there is an opportunity to reinvent oneself for the future of all if we leverage developing projects and focus on future economies through STEM education and entrepreneurship. And from the ashes, a new day will emerge. A day of promise. A day of hope. A day in the future when we will all live in one barrio on a Silicon Island for all.

In this book Frank and I will discuss with Latino leaders from the pinnacles of industries what diversity and inclusion look like. We will discuss the milestones that must be achieved to reach a truly diverse and equitable society. We will remind Latinos from all walks of life that it is their inherent talent and skills that add value to enterprise and is the power that will continue to drive the engine of innovation.

We will provide the framework for corporations, governments, and individuals to build a more inclusive future in every industry by leveraging Hispanic ingenuity, skill, and innovation for a better future for all. We will show Latinos how to take that road less traveled and how that will make all the difference.

—**José Morey**
Caguas, Puerto Rico
September 2021

INTRODUCTION: THE LATINO DIGITAL LEADERSHIP MODEL

This book is a result of a series of interviews with Latino/ Latinx leaders from Frank's first book, *Building the Latino Future*, who now expand on the evolution of Latino digital intelligence. We will show some of the key challenges facing the Latino community, and the common thread running through each of them, in elements based on seven principles — Decision Making, Intelligence, Game Plan, Inclusion, Technology, Abundance, and Leverage (DIGITAL).

Each letter of the DIGITAL Model represents what a great leader needs to possess, especially in the age of the digital evolution. The seven elements that make up the acronym DIGITAL appear as chapters in the book; but, as we are taking a new and innovated approach, they are considered evolution sections, as the purpose of this book is to see our contributions through an evolutionary process.

Combined strengths can be used as guidelines, and used to illustrate each element that leads the Latino community through evolutionary growth, but it also shows the common challenges Latinos face on their academic and professional journey. However, some of the practices and strategies to succeed have been through participation in a digital economy. It is with their skills with personal, transactional, and user-generated data that these individuals have excelled in corporate platforms and in diverse sectors. Also, it is important to share, a core element for growth in the venture capital sector, which is why we add Digital Citizenship for the "Evolution of Latino Digital Intelligence."

An effective Latino digital leader will be aware of business goals, such as in the industries covered in this book, and will learn from corporate America, venture capital, the nonprofit sector, academia, media, the arts, the technology sector. Latinx leaders under 30 know their job responsibilities support the continued evolution. The following describes the framework for DIGITAL.

DECISION MAKING: LATINOS AT THE TABLE – CHAPTER I

We will share stories from corporate America to the boardroom. If Latinos are not invited to the table, we as a community will find ways to get to the table and build and create our own table.

Although these sections are labeled chapters, they are better known as evolution sections. This first evolution can be dealt with both organizationally and at an individual level; thus, you will read about these executives developing leadership skills. Great leaders must develop the ability to become great decision-makers, possess emotional intelligence, be able to handle uncertainty and become more tenacious, and through these experiences will naturally transform to gain intuition and provide honesty and integrity at the boardroom table. They will provide due diligence research and include the stories of the great Latino and Latina executives. All of these folks possess these traits:

- Confidence
- Inspire others with authenticity
- Commitment and passion for their craft
- Good communicator, with full transparency
- Decision-making capabilities, at high-pressure levels

INTELLIGENCE: INTELLIGENCE WILL PUSH YOU THROUGH – CHAPTER 2

In this second evolution stage, we share the stories of influential Latinos and Latinas in the healthcare industry, from physicians to hospital executives. During the times of the pandemic and postpandemic, an evolutionary set of traits that will propel us into the future includes levels of intelligence and emotional connection that will make every person feel empowered. The levels that are key are empathy, motivation, and authentic self.

All physicians and digital leaders practice these traits of intelligence to evolve in the twenty-first century and beyond.

The forms of evolution in DIGITAL Intelligence are:

- Empathy: Physicians practice body language to show forms of understanding and authenticity. Provide signs to empower others. For leaders, having empathy is critical to managing a successful team or organization. Leaders with empathy have the ability to put themselves in someone else's situation. They help develop the people on their team, challenge others who are acting unfairly, give constructive feedback, and listen to those who need to be heard.

- Self-awareness is another key element to strengthen leadership. Through these stories, you will gain insight and learn about humility.

GAME PLAN: THE GAME PLAN IS THE ACTION – CHAPTER 3

Think about your final goal. It might be a project you are working on, or a long-term vision that will continue to develop and evolve. In this section, interviewees are rising stars under 30. What is it you and your team are playing for? Picture it clearly in your mind. Most sports champions will tell you that the more clearly you envision success, the more likely it is to happen. There are really two components to your game plan.

A game plan is also known as how you define your culture. For example, currently many companies are incorporating Latinx as part of their company culture, and in this section interviewees under the age of 30 have been selected to share their leadership traits with Gen Z and beyond. Therefore, as a leader you first need to understand and appreciate your role, and how your influence impacts the company culture. However, it is imperative that guidance and mentoring are established early on as part of one's game plan.

As part of the game plan, we must always remember that motivation comes and goes, but inspiration is what keeps people engaged. The great leadership styles you will read about in our book are these Latinx leaders who were prepared to tackle any challenge, which led to productivity in their chosen industry.

INCLUSION: INCLUSION DEVELOPS NEW LEADERSHIP – CHAPTER 4

In this evolution section, you read about some of the greatest Latino and Latina nonprofit and educational leaders in the United States, and you will gain understanding through the stories of how all have faced challenges before and during the COVID-19 pandemic, the kinds of leadership challenges and uncertainties they have faced. These insightful stories give us a new grip on how to strengthen and develop the unique leadership patterns of engagement that drive inclusion, which makes you acutely aware of how some past patterns and complex experiences support your work and develop leadership traits.

If you are a leader looking for higher levels of awareness and performance in your role, then this may well be your next step.

TECHNOLOGY: TECHNOLOGY IS A WAY OF LIFE – CHAPTER 5

The leaders in this evolution section will provide stories and insights into the empowering steps they took to be the first or a pioneer in technology as leaders to connect their practices, policies, and procedures to innovation.

It is imperative to share various roles of Latino and Latina technology leaders within schools and districts across the country. These principles are predicated on a core belief that in a Future Ready school, all students have equitable access to qualified technology leaders. As you will read in many of our stories, the interviewees did not have equitable rights; therefore, many had to be the pioneers as first-generation graduates and individuals in technology to fight for the equal rights for technology, whether it was internet access or access to capital.

- It is an imperative by asking the most common question: What will create a digital evolution for the Latinx community?
- What will create an environment that has instructional leadership and support with technological fluency and background in this field?
- How do we create online networks that support the educational and professional learning collaboration efforts to support disenfranchised schools?

ABUNDANCE: ABUNDANCE OF LIFE – CHAPTER 6

In this evolution section, you will learn stories of Latinos and Latinas in the media and the arts who are sharing stories through innovation, and helping create the narrative through growth in becoming a collaborative individual. The folks in the media and arts are sharing success stories that highlight ways of having an abundant attitude, through their focus of becoming successful.

An abundant attitude is a work in progress. As a Latino community we all learn how to contribute to growth and the abundance in our community.

———

LEVERAGE: LEVERAGE PROVIDES ENERGY TO MAKE IT HAPPEN – CHAPTER 7

In the evolution section, you will learn about entrepreneurs and venture capitalists who have made their way through gaining leverage. The motivation behind the actions in the stories you will read about may vary, but the common thread is all have been the first moving toward this new frontier as a Latinx community and have concentrated on innovation return on investment (ROI), one of them being the fact that funding an innovative start-up and acquiring it (or its technology) later is more economical than developing the equivalent talent in-house.

In this evolution section, you will read about Leverage Leadership principles that have proven to be a successful framework to streamline and implement when investing in the Latinx future.

1

Decision Making
C-Suite Level Leaders and Board Directors

Ramiro Cavazos
President and CEO
United States Hispanic Chamber of Commerce (USHCC)
Teamwork and partnering with others is essential for achieving success and establishing a win-win relationship.
— Ramiro Cavazos

RAMIRO CAVAZOS WAS BORN IN McAllen, Texas, and raised in Weslaco in the Rio Grande Valley. His grandparents, one of the pioneer families who settled Weslaco in 1919, founded one of the town's first grocery stores.

While his parents both attended college, he was the first child in his generation to graduate from college.

Ramiro was fortunate to grow up the oldest of four children. His father was a rancher, farmer, and elected official, and his mother was a bookkeeper for an automobile dealer and later an aloe vera producer and distributor, and they were considered a middle-income family. Ramiro was able to attend college based on an academic scholarship he received from the University of Texas at Austin. He also received a little bit of financial help from his parents and worked part-time while attending school.

Ramiro's biggest obstacle to getting to college and succeeding was that he did not have a strong network of high school classmates to lean on for support when he moved away to go to college. He felt that he did not have a core group of friends from growing up that allowed him to have a foundation of support as he progressed through life.

Ramiro was able to complete his undergraduate degree in three years by receiving additional credit for certain coursework and attending summer school in between semesters.

Ramiro's parents raised their children to be hard workers and to never give up, and therefore he was able to keep moving forward in spite of any challenges.

There is no question that there is a widening gap between the "haves" and "have-nots" in America's economy. Because of this, the United States Hispanic Chamber of Commerce (USHCC) is working hard to create wealth and prosperity for close to 5 million Hispanic-owned businesses.

Many of our communities in the United States live in low-income communities with limited means and resources, and many live in areas where it is difficult to access quality food, capital, or the internet. The digital divide has become wider because of the impact of COVID-19 on the economy and the lack of investment by corporate and political leaders who have not prioritized Latino communities' needs and strengths.

In fact, many school districts and local municipal governments overseen by Hispanic leaders have limited their budgets, typically targeting education and basic municipal services, and allocated funds to the construction of cell phone and internet towers. Public housing authorities have also made investments to expand digital and internet resources for young people who live with their parents or grandparents in public housing so that they may have access to high-speed internet and Wi-Fi in order for them to do their homework or for their parents to apply for jobs or to run their own start-up businesses where there hasn't been access to the internet in the past.

The COVID-19 pandemic coincided with the harsh winter weather in 2021 and a year of significant civil rights protests that all combined to expose the disparities that exist within American communities for Hispanic and low-income Americans, who struggle with basic needs, such as access to healthcare, affordable housing, good jobs, good education, and access to the internet and digital resources, including laptops and computers.

In order to be at the decision-making table, more Latinos and Latinas need to serve on city councils, housing authority boards, school district boards, city boards/commissions, and higher offices in order to be at the decision-making table where investments in technological equipment are being made using public dollars. These leaders can help to prioritize inner-city neighborhoods, older commercial corridors, predominantly Hispanic residential areas, and low-income markets that need allies and champions in the seats of power at all levels – not just local, but also state and federal – in order to make decisions that prioritize the needs of Hispanic communities. Ramiro would also encourage more Latinos and Latinas to consider running for elected office, where we are widely underrepresented at the local, state, and federal levels.

Ramiro represents the United States Hispanic Chamber of Commerce as its president and CEO. It is a very proud national network of more than 260 Hispanic Chambers of Commerce that are located across the country . . . from Honolulu, Hawaii, to Rhode Island . . . from Seattle, Washington, to Puerto Rico . . . and from the state of Wisconsin bordering Canada all the way to the magical Rio Grande Valley of South Texas.

Each of these Hispanic Chambers serves as an economic oasis of information and opportunity for the more than 5 million Hispanic-owned businesses in each of their areas. All of these businesses and Hispanic Chambers are working hard to increase the number of contracts awarded to Latino entrepreneurs from Fortune 1000 companies, the U.S. government purchasing programs, and local and regional marketplaces. These businesses represent uniquely talented, multilingual, and ambitious Hispanics who wish to be successful. These entrepreneurs understand that they need to compete on a global scale through international trade, including imports and exports.

Prior to COVID-19, many of these small businesses were challenged by not being invited to be at the important tables where decision making and authority are shared. Because of COVID and the need to survive with limited access to capital, many of these businesses have reinvented themselves and have adjusted in order to operate in new digital, virtual, and changing marketplaces. This evolution has been brought about by the pandemic, systemic race and discrimination challenges, climate change, infrastructure hurdles, and the growing gap in broadband access.

The USHCC is working hard to open doors of opportunity with Fortune 1000 firms and the U.S. government and leverage private sector resources to reinvest directly to small Hispanic Business Enterprises (HBEs) through capital grants, supporting our Hispanic Chambers through chamber support grants, and utilizing our website by providing technical assistance and helpful guidelines to access Paycheck Protection Program (PPP) resources and many other tools that can augment the availability of capital and broadband/technology/Wi-Fi access in order to be more competitive during these challenging virtual times.

Ramiro indicated that there are three main opportunities needed for Latinos and Latinas to succeed in growing their businesses and creating wealth and prosperity as hardworking entrepreneurs in America.

The number-one need for any business, especially Latino and Latina-owned businesses, is access to diverse capital through debt, equity, and other types of investment/financing. Historically, our businesses have not been awarded access to loans at the same percentage as non-Latino-owned businesses, which we work hard every day to improve through our relationships with America's large financial institutions, community banks, the U.S. Treasury and Federal Reserve Bank, financial technology firms (fintechs), community lenders, Community Development Financial Institutions (CDFIs), and other institutions.

The second area of greatest need to grow Hispanic businesses is access to a competitive environment with Fortune 1000 firms, the U.S. government's purchases, and through free trade without tariffs through importing and exporting products and services to an international customer base. Latino- and Latina-owned businesses have not been given the same opportunities to have access to contracts and business from many of the same buyers of goods and services as compared to non-Latino-owned businesses. There is availability and a high level of talent and customer service among Hispanic entrepreneurs, and they must be given the same place at the corporate and U.S. government tables where decision-makers of all types of purchases embrace Hispanic-owned businesses.

The third opportunity that is needed to grow Latino- and Latina-owned businesses is capacity building, training, mentorship, and coaching. Historically, non-Latino and Latina-owned businesses have not had the access to resources that provide support systems, mentorship, and inherited relationships. These businesses must be given the same tools and the ability to use them by the same support systems that have traditionally rewarded businesses throughout this country seeking to achieve the American dream.

These three components are necessary for any business to grow. At the USHCC, Ramiro indicated that they are working hard to make the connections, to provide more capital, and build more capacity for our Latino and Latina-owned businesses through this programming.

Esther Aguilera
CEO
Latino Corporate Directors Association

Never underestimate the resiliency and drive of the Latino community in the United States.

— Esther Aguilera

THE DIGITAL DIVIDE AND COVID: A TALE OF TWO REALITIES

The pandemic of 2020, which has extended into 2021, has laid bare a tale of two realities: the inequities of U.S. society. It is a time to contemplate Esther Aguilera's humble, immigrant roots and the reality of today's families, struggling to make ends meet while trying to live with dignity during a pandemic. At the same time, there is a resolve to persevere with the strength of Latino values and ethos.

Esther's immigrant story is a tale of two lands. Esther came to the United States from Jalisco, Mexico. Her mother hired a coyote to facilitate their travel across the border to the United States. Esther was four years old and one of six children; her mother sought to bring the family together with Esther's father, who was applying for U.S. citizenship at the time. After they crossed the border, they reunited with her father, and she was raised in San Fernando, California.

Esther's father's mother, Rufina Perez, was a U.S. citizen from Colorado. Her family had lived in Colorado for many generations, from the time before it became a part of the United States. Esther's grandmother married a Mexican national, Bernardino Aguilera, and, just as the Great Depression set in, following the market crash of 1929, her husband was deported. She was forced to choose between staying with her family in Colorado or leaving her country to join her husband on his journey back to Mexico. They were swept up as part of the Mexican Repatriation, "a mass deportation of Mexicans and Mexican-Americans from the United States between 1929 and 1936. Estimates of how many were repatriated range from 400,000 to 2,000,000. An estimated 60 percent of those deported were birthright citizens of the United States," as reported in Wikipedia. Based on historical accounts "many Mexicans and U.S. citizens of Mexican origin endured "harassment, beatings, and heavy-handed tactics."

In short, although Esther's father had a legitimate claim to citizenship, there was a process that lasted more than 10 years before he secured citizenship that allowed her mother, as well as all six children, to obtain green cards.

Esther and her five siblings formed close ties as their father labored in landscaping and their mother took jobs as an occasional worker in the garment industry to make ends meet. While times were tough, her family did not access public assistance or food stamps even after they attained residency. Public education and free school lunches helped them get by. The desire to advance is what drove all six Aguilera children to complete college. Esther studied public policy at Occidental College in Los Angeles, California, before landing her first job in Washington, DC.

In Esther's 30-year career in Washington, DC she had the distinct honor of working alongside the nation's most powerful leaders of every sector, from members of Congress to cabinet members to national nonprofit and association leaders and to top corporate executives, as well as organizing meetings and events with U.S. presidents.

Esther's path to Washington, DC, was unexpected. After graduating from Occidental College with distinction with a public policy major, she landed her first job as a policy associate with the Nation Council of La Raza in 1990 (now known as UnidosUS). For Esther's next role, she worked at the U.S. Capital for six years, starting as legislative assistant and then as executive director of the Congressional Hispanic Caucus – the entity at the seat of power in the nation's Capital. To say that she felt the "imposter's syndrome" is an understatement. She was an immigrant girl, not yet a citizen but a permanent resident, driving the legislative agenda to advance opportunities and equity for Latinos in all social, business, and economic spheres of policy.

Esther mentions that she was not exposed to politics or economic markets at the kitchen table while growing up. The Latino characteristics of resiliency and adapting were helpful yet again in enabling her to learn quickly, on the job, with top leaders all around her to learn from.

A consistent thread in Esther's personal and professional pursuits has been a commitment to elevating Latinos to positions of power and helping them to claim their seats at the decision-making table.

For 11 years, Esther led the Congressional Hispanic Caucus Institute (CHCI) as president and CEO. CHCI is known as the nation's premier Latino youth leadership development organization, providing hands-on paid internships, fellowships, and week-long training at the seat of power in the nation's Capital for high school, college, and graduate students. During her tenure, she tripled the organization's operating funds, including leading a capital campaign that raised $7 million toward the purchase of the headquarters building. The increase in funds meant that CHCI reached more students. While it once served 50 students annually, at the time by her departure in 2015, the organization had 1,600 students involved in various leadership programs annually.

Today, as president and CEO of the Latino Corporate Directors Association (LCDA), Esther exercises her influence with some of the most powerful companies by bringing together accomplished executives at the pinnacle of corporate governance to advance diversity in the boardroom. Her focus is to drive an increase in the representation of Latinos at the decision-making tables of corporate America.

Esther is on a mission to connect qualified Latinos with forward-thinking companies with a business case: No company can be effectively governed without Latinos at the decision-making table. Latinos are the current and future customers of companies as well as the employees driving their business success, and their numbers are only growing. If a company is not connected and engaged, it is losing market share.

The number of Latinos on boards is small, only 2.2 percent of the board seats among the Russell 3000 Index publicly traded companies, far behind the community's nearly 20 percent representation in the total U.S. population. Esther states that she continues to hear the excuse that companies can't find qualified Latinos. With a growing LCDA network, there is proof of an ample supply, and that excuse no longer applies.

Latino leaders of nonprofit organizations are the unsung heroes of our nation. Rarely is this talented cohort of leaders recognized by the mainstream nonprofit sector for their exceptional strategic and results-focused organizational missions. Many Latino nonprofit leaders build multifaceted organizations that drive social change.

Esther has been at the intersection of public, private, nonprofit, and government sectors and draws on the vast opportunities and strategies to leverage growth and impact for the Hispanic population. All in all, she brings three decades of experience to organizations focused on gaining recognition for the growing Hispanic population of the United States and ensuring that members of that group attain positions of leadership.

One of the biggest obstacles to success is access to foundational resources and investments to build the nonprofit institutions that support the advancement of U.S. Latinos, the second largest demographic group in the nation, and make America strong.

The discussion about the digital divide today is also a tale of two realities. The differences have been exacerbated by the devastating impact of the COVID-19 pandemic. The economic standing of Black and Brown communities was impacted disproportionately by the global financial crisis of 2008. They were barely rebounding when the COVID-19 pandemic hit, devastating the economy, lives, and livelihoods. Again, Brown and Black communities have experienced a disproportionate impact.

Pandemics know no borders or county lines. COVID-19 has been an equal opportunity destroyer. In 2020, the Latino Corporate Directors Association teamed up with McKinsey & Company to report on "the impact of COVID on the lives and livelihood of U.S. Latinos."

According to the McKinsey September 2020 report, U.S. Latinos have borne a disproportionate share of the pandemic's health and economic damage. Why? The report found that Latinos are more likely to work in essential roles and more likely to know people who have suffered or died from the disease. As a result, according to the analysis by McKinsey:

- Latinos are also about three times as likely to be infected with COVID-19.
- Latinos account for 51.3 percent of deaths from the disease.
- Latinos are 1.5 to 2 times more at risk of economic disruption. The economic consequences of COVID-19 will likely disrupt all stages of Latinos' wealth-building journey.
- The five business sectors most affected by the pandemic also represent almost 50 percent of revenues for Hispanic- and Latino-owned businesses.

Esther was contemplating what her experience would be like if she were in her teenage years in the current pandemic times, and living in the difficult socioeconomic conditions of the California barrio of San Fernando. Her father's seasonal landscaping job meant that winters were times of scarcity – of food, heat, and rent money. The eight members of the family lived in a two-bedroom, one-bath rental. The socio-economic conditions of this kind of upbringing are a reality for many families and teenagers today.

First, in terms of education, even with free Wi-Fi access and a Google Chrome book provided by her school, Esther cannot imagine having the space and privacy for six siblings to meaningfully participate in their different classes every day. Public libraries were few and, based on a Google search today, three of four free public libraries in San Fernando were temporarily closed during the pandemic. Plus, Latino households have higher rates of multigenerational living arrangements, bringing babies, youth, parents, and grandparents under one roof, causing even higher levels of noise and chaos.

Esther indicates that if she were a student today, a teen with low self-esteem, signing in virtually for class from home, it would cause agony and distress. She would have been mortified to share her home surroundings, knowing that the overcrowded living quarters would be on full view. Money was so stretched that new clothes were a luxury.

With so many social pressures on teenagers today, Esther worries that the high rate of suicides among teens has only increased in a time of distance isolation, social-media unreality, and self-loathing and shame about meager living conditions.

Parentology cited a study from the *Journal of the American Academy of Child and Adolescent Psychiatry* (JAACAP) that concluded that children and adolescents are experiencing higher rates of depression and anxiety resulting from the required isolation and loneliness of COVID-19. "Adolescence has always been a risky time, but the latest CDC survey shows teen suicide rates, suicide attempts, and suicidal ideation are on the rise . . . Throw a pandemic into the throes of adolescence and you have a recipe for anxiety, stress, and possible suicide risk," notes Jenny Heitz, the author of the article.

A pre-COVID, 2018 HipLatina article cited the Center for Disease Control and Prevention (CDC) 2015 survey on youth high-risk behavior, which reported that "15 percent of Latina adolescents in the U.S. have attempted suicide. That number is much higher when compared to 9.8 percent and 10.2 percent for white and black female teens, respectively. Furthermore, almost 26 percent of Latina teens considered suicide."

What is more, for Latino citizens over 65, with even less knowledge and connection to the internet, access to COVID vaccines poses a huge threat. Seniors must rely on finding and registering to receive the vaccine, which requires long hours of maneuvering through a website. One advantage for elders in multigenerational homes is that their grandchildren may help them to navigate, in their view, the "wild-wide-web."

Even with the chaos and devastation, the Latino spirit and resiliency stands the test of time in weathering the tale of two realities. The road to recovery in the United States leads through Latino communities, the economic engine of the economy. Latinos not only count for 2 of every 10 Americans, the population is growing on an average of 1 million year-over-year. Latinos contribute 25 percent of the U.S. gross domestic product (GDP) and represent 82 percent of new entrants to the workforce, making them drivers of U.S. economic growth and productivity.

Jesus Mantas
Senior Managing Partner
IBM

It's easier to tech an engineer to sell, than to teach a seller to be an engineer: Content and mastery matters.

— Anonymous

Who you are in the minds of other people depends mostly on how you are perceived by them, and that is typically different from how you see yourself.

— Jesus Mantas

Jesus grew up in Granada, Spain, and was a first-generation university graduate in his family. He began working as a technology consultant in the south of Spain at age 13, while still in high school. The career he chose wasn't taught at any university in the south of Spain, so he had to leave his family home and move to Madrid at the age of 17. His parents worked hard to save enough to fund Jesus's six-year university degree. Fortunately, he grew up in Spain, where the public education system was very good, and his university tuition was less than $500 per year; the main cost for him was the cost of living in an unfamiliar city.

Hispanics represent 18.5 percent of the U.S. population, yet only 4 percent of the executive ranks. Hispanics are the fastest growing and youngest minority in the United States. And yet despite the advantages of size, power, and youth there is still a huge lack of Hispanic leaders.

IBM has created P-TECH schools, where students earn combined high school and associate degrees in technology. P-TECH includes 77 U.S. school districts that are predominantly Hispanic. Jesus personally increased his commitment to advocate for making Hispanic diversity a business imperative by mentoring Hispanics, advancing them to leadership positions, and investing in Hispanic entrepreneurs.

Jesus stresses that we all have a responsibility to support Hispanic education, workforce opportunities, and leadership, not only for the benefit of Hispanics but for the entire country. Jesus believes that when we work to help this generation do well, it will lift economic opportunity for everyone – not only Hispanics. No other demographic can pick up the slack if we don't. Success may require that we make these issues not only Hispanic issues but broader U.S. societal and economic issues, including more allies in the actions.

Jesus is a senior managing partner in IBM Global Business Services, a $17 billion unit of IBM. He is responsible for global strategy, offering portfolio and corporate development, and he also focuses on technologies that impact society, such as artificial intelligence (AI) and quantum computing. Jesus cochairs IBM's Hispanic Diversity Council, which promotes programs around education, mentorship, and creating advancement opportunities for Hispanics. Jesus is also a board member at Biogen, Inc., a S&P 500 biotechnology company, and serves in the World Economic Forum Global AI Council.

In Jesus's view there are two critical skills that fuel the digital age: data science (including AI) and design.

Data is the fuel that powers the modern digital transformations – and data science is the fundamental skillset required to understand, manage, and benefit from that fuel. If data is the fuel, AI is the engine, and therefore data science includes both the preparation and understanding of the data, as well as the algorithms that create value from it.

Design is at the heart of optimizing the human-technology interfaces, to ensure that people adopt and benefit from technology. Tons of data and algorithms without proper design that ensures adoption and application often don't succeed.

Jesus credits education, mentors, family, role models, and luck as the factors that contributed to his success, and research shows this is a common set of factors for others as well. In each of these areas, many Latinxs have obstacles:

- On the topic of education, not every Latinx can afford – or is interested in – a college degree, but that should not be a limiting factor for them to learn and practice the skills that will make them successful in technology jobs. A few models are emerging, like P-TECH, and persuading tech companies to hire for skills and not for degrees, but much more needs to be done.
- Mentoring is an area that most mention as a key to success, but in Jesus's view there are two obstacles: Latinxs are less mentored than other communities in the United States, and even those who have a mentor are typically "over-mentored bur under-sponsored." Active advocacy and sponsorship is a critical obstacle to hiring more Hispanics in technology roles.
- Family environment is a key influence on young Hispanics' choices and successes in jobs and careers,

and therefore the limited penetration of Latinxs in technology companies perpetuates a limited family influence for the next generations.

- Role models create belief and inspire people to aim high. The lack of role models in the eyes of Latinx puts them on a disadvantage as they "can't be what they can't see." The Latinx community needs more relatable role models, inspiring graduates to lean into technology careers.

Jesus tells us that if our economy is to thrive, we need increased representation in leadership roles across all industries – and definitely in technology.

As part of its research into people and development, the IBM Institute for Business Value recently surveyed Hispanics in the United States. One key finding is that professional advancement opportunities have played a crucial role in helping senior Hispanic executives achieve their success. But the survey also shows that younger leaders are not getting those advancement opportunities:

- Only 30 percent of junior managers say they have access to mentorship programs or on-the-job training.
- Only 20 percent say they are empowered to overcome their professional challenges.
- Most worrying, 67 percent say that they have to work harder to succeed because of their Hispanic identity.

The most important action we need to take is to make Hispanic representation a clear business priority, with operational accountability, and prepare Hispanic communities for the future of work, taking into account the inherent diversity of the Hispanic and Latino populations in the United States, and personalizing the engagement programs to "meet Latinos where they are" in their journeys.

Make Hispanic leadership representation a business priority	Make Hispanic leadership representation a company performance priority	Identify a leadership pipeline and path for progression	Implement active advocacy programs, in addition to mentorship
Prepare Hispanics for the "future of work"	Enable entry-level and experienced Hispanics for the shift to digitization	Activate public private partnerships to develop skills at scale	Change company policies to hire for skills rather than degrees
Design for Hispanic heterogeneity and personalized actions	Simplify messages and actions to match Hispanics priorities	Meet Hispanics where they are in their life and work journeys	Reflect subcultures in programs seeking Hispanic adoption

This is the link to the full study: https://www.ibm.com/thought-leadership/institute-business-value/report/hispanic-talent-advantage.

Victor Arias
Managing Director and Partner in Charge
Dallas/Fort Worth Office at Diversified Search

> Touch the money! Nothing wrong with staff roles but they
> are normally looked at with "cost center" lenses. Instead,
> go create tangible revenue for your enterprise.
>
> – Victor Arias

Victor Arias grew up in El Paso, Texas, as a child of the
second generation in the United States, which he mentions
doesn't count for much in El Paso. Many families maintain
their traditional language and customs. Victor grew up
speaking Spanish as his first language with many *costum-*
bres (customs) *mexicanas queridas*. A large extended family
also mean lots of *misas* (church masses), *celebraciones*
(celebrations), *taquizas, canciones* (songs), and so on.

Victor was a first-generation college student and went to
UTEP in El Paso, which kept the family intact (Victor feels,
as many others do, that the close-knit family can be an
obstacle initially for many Latinos). Victor was fortunate
to succeed academically and always knew he wanted something more, and had his eye on graduate school – although
he wasn't sure what that meant. *La mano de Dios* (the hand
of God) guided him to a conference room where he met
the assistant admissions director to the Stanford Graduate
School of Business, who convinced him to apply. Victor
received his acceptance while working at a bank (he
worked as a secretary), and the rest is history. Victor told
the credit manager, his boss, who after getting over his

incredulity, told the bank president, who called Victor into his office. There are many guardian angels along life's path and Art Gonzales was one of those.

The president of the bank asked Jesus lots of questions and finally felt he had permission to give some advice. He proposed that even though Jesus had the opportunity to go straight to Stanford upon graduation from UTEP, he could defer the guaranteed admission for two years and start working in the management training program at the bank in the meantime. Eventually, Victor took over the credit manager role prior to heading off to Stanford, and Victor is convinced that this experience propelled him to greater heights and also to complete an MBA at Stanford.

After earning his MBA at Stanford, Victor took a job at the Houston headquarters of the same bank that he started with in El Paso. After one and a half years and the birth of a new baby son, Victor was recruited by LaSalle Partners in Chicago. Among about one hundred employees, Victor was the first Latino and probably one of three people of color in the company. He recalls that it was a fantastic experience and that he learned a great deal. One of those lessons was how to become chameleon-like and change himself to match different situation. Victor felt he couldn't be his Latino self. Whenever Victor ran into a Latino-looking person in a suit in the financial district, he would stop him and engage in conversation.

It was then that Victor met another gentleman in Houston who was establishing the National Society of Hispanic MBAs. They recruited other founders and completed the formation of the organization and secured its nonprofit 501(c)(3) status. After one and a half years of meetings, they kicked off the organization. Victor was in charge of chapter development and also ran the first five national conferences. Victor then became the national president and asked LaSalle Partners to donate office space, which they kindly agreed to.

The national office remained there until about 1992, when it was relocated to Dallas. Victor also relocated to Dallas in 1993 but kept his distance to allow others the opportunity to get involved and take leadership roles. Victor has stayed tangentially involved and has been helping the current CEO with advice and some webinars on preparing for board service for the group's members.

In many respects, Latinos have led the way in the adoption of technology, especially with mobile technology, where they overindex in usage. This has opened up once unattainable areas of communication and data where Latinos previously experienced real challenges. However, mobile phones are the tip of the untouched iceberg. Laptops and desktops are the key tools utilized all the way up the food chain, from very young preschoolers to corporate executives. The ability to innovate around data and technology is the norm today, and yet Latinos have been left behind. The reasons for this range from lack of internet connectivity to the costs of acquiring cutting-edge technology and tools, which can be prohibitive. The key to fixing this is to pressure telecom and connectivity companies to provide more and better service to underserved areas and also to convince consumer-tech companies to create much broader access for underserved communities in an effort to train more of the nation's future workforce. After all, Latinos represent the largest sector of growth for the future workforce. Last, the largest economic opportunity for all companies is the consumption potential of Latinos . . . which should be a great motivation for companies to get on board.

Latinos are shareholders, board members, and influencers who can "educate" these companies and convince them to take appropriate actions.

Jesus advises, "Be the best at what you do! You can't be everything to everybody so don't try to be something you're not. In that vein, be the top subject matter expert in your company and also tie back your activities to the revenue stream of the company. How do you influence revenue growth?

"Touch the money! Nothing wrong with staff roles but they are normally looked at with 'cost center' lenses. Instead, go create tangible revenue for your enterprise.

"Get heavily involved with nonprofit boards and not just as board members but as leading them or leading committees. You will get noticed by others who are already on corporate boards or influence their decisions."

Thaddeus Arroyo
Chief Executive Officer
AT&T Consumer, AT&T Communications, LLC
at AT&T

> The way to realize your potential is to be a continuous learner, embrace technology, and think forward with an eye on what's possible. Through education, hard work, and perseverance, great things can happen.
>
> – Thaddeus Arroyo

Thaddeus Arroyo's life has been an interesting and often unexpected journey. He never could have anticipated being where he is today. His father emigrated from Spain and his mother is the daughter of Mexican immigrants. Thaddeus was born in San Francisco and spent most of his formative years in the Dallas area. As a naturalized U.S. citizen, his father instilled in him a sense of responsibility for embracing all of the opportunities this country afforded, such as a public education.

After high school, Thaddeus chose to pursue a college degree in mathematics and computer science, placing a bet on the skills he believed would be the most relevant in the future. One of the obstacles he faced was this decision and need to embrace and welcome the unknown. He took a calculated risk and invested himself in becoming a first-generation college graduate with the expectation that a technology career would one day help him provide for a family.

When Thaddeus graduated from high school, students didn't have easy access to computers. He chose to pursue a career in information technology without having grown up with a computer in his house. Over the past several decades there has been tremendous progress in creating hard-to-imagine experiences enabled by businesses connecting to consumers in ever-evolving ways. Thaddeus considers it an honor to be a part of this digital evolution.

Thaddeus states that the nation's industries must work to expand affordable access to these networks and to all those who need access to gain competitive employment, to learn and to engage in digitally relevant ways. Thaddeus believes we must open new doors to digitally fueled experiences for communities – including the entire Latinx community. Those looking to be part of this change must lean in and make their voices heard. The best way to be at the decision-making table is to share how the power of connectivity has positively impacted each person's life and can do the same for others.

It's also important to understand that our modern economy requires new skills as we move deep into the heart of the fourth industrial revolution. In 2016, the World Economic Forum noted that in many industries and countries, the most in-demand occupations or specialties did not exist 10 or even 5 years ago. Furthermore, 65 percent of the jobs that Latinos may do in the future don't even exist today.

Thaddeus has seen first-hand the truly disruptive nature that connecting people to the internet can have on society. Mobile internet via cell phone technology has served as an engine for economic growth in the United States. Mobile is the potential that emerges in virtually any connected society.

Thaddeus has always been passionate about technology and aspired to be in a position where he could one day make positive, meaningful impact in his career, like so many who invested in his development.

Thaddeus started his career in the IT department of Southwestern Bell, which was located in the building just across the street from his office today. Soon after, he worked at Sabre Corporation, where he gained valuable experience in both technology and business operations. This propelled his career journey into leadership roles, where he was fortunate to have the opportunity to hold diverse executive positions, including CIO of Cingular Wireless, CIO of AT&T, CEO of AT&T Mexico, and CEO of AT&T Business, before becoming CEO of AT&T Consumer.

Throughout these experiences, Thaddeus found that leaders must innovate and evolve to meet the changing needs of their customers and teams in order to maintain relevancy and find success. One way to do this is by establishing a set of fundamental values and then putting them into action. These values start with fostering an inclusive culture so that you have diverse perspectives that reflect and represent the customers you serve. Thaddeus is proud of the work AT&T has done in this area.

Creating an inclusive culture that is diverse in backgrounds, experience, and thought is truly a never-ending journey. As Latino lives continue to shift to an increasingly digitally driven world, we're able to unlock more opportunities to engage in diversity and inclusion through the power of instant connectivity. Businesses must tap into these capabilities to fully realize their inclusivity aspirations.

Thaddeus feels fortunate to be part of a diverse community of organizations making meaningful changes for the communities they serve. He serves on the board of directors of Global Payments as Director and Technology Committee Chair. He is also honored to serve on the board of the National Center for Women & Information Technology (NCWIT) and SMU Cox School of Business Executive Advisory Board. Additionally, he also serves as a trustee for the Dallas Museum of Art.

Hispanic leaders continue to emerge as prominent figures throughout corporate America. A key part of being a business leader is managing the moments that matter to your teams, customers, and the communities you identify with and serve. This is especially true when facing adversity. Adversity gives leaders a chance to build confidence and engagement with teams as well as an opportunity to grow your business by leaning into change and embracing disruptive capabilities. The Latinx community has demonstrated a unique ability to embrace change and digitally driven experiences. This capability is critical to being able to innovate and lead in the moments that matter.

Success begins with saying "yes" to new challenges. Thaddeus believes Latinos need to catch themselves when fear or uncertainty arise. This is something Thaddeus has faced in his career with every shift that seemed unnatural or uncomfortable. Anyone aspiring to grow their career should remember that success is less about being the leader and more about magnifying individual strengths within the team. It's about empowering people and making sure they feel understood, valued, and appreciated.

Since 1996, U.S. broadband providers have invested nearly $2 trillion to connect Hispanic communities. Over the past five years (2016–2020), AT&T's total investment in the United States, including capital investment and acquisitions of spectrum and wireless operations, was more than $105 billion.

This private investment has provided most American consumers good experiences over some of the world's best connectivity networks. Today, even more people are working and learning from home. Society has seen the emergence of the largest remote workforce and education system in the history of the world. This all happened in response to a global pandemic. This has forever changed the relevancy for connectivity. The increased number of digitally enhanced and digital-first experiences has created a growing need for reliable high-speed connectivity. However, today's networks don't reach everyone, and it will take multiple industries as well as the government working together to solve this challenge.

AT&T supports the Federal Communication Commission's (FCC's) efforts to expand broadband access to many parts of rural America through the Rural Digital Opportunity Fund and Digital Opportunity Data Collection. AT&T is also committed to growing affordable access to broadband connectivity for all customers and all communities.

When he was young, Thaddeus's mother shared a simple motto with him – *sin limites*. To her, it means never limiting your opportunities with self-imposed perceptions or barriers that can ultimately be overcome. Over the years, Thaddeus would like to believe that he has incorporated this belief into his own leadership style and the lessons he has shared with others. Thaddeus thinks this phrase could serve as a powerful mantra for many. As technology and connectivity remove the physical barriers of our world, the only limits that begin to exist are the limits that we place upon ourselves or upon our teams, based on our own self-perceived limitations.

Myrna Soto
Chief Strategy and Trust Officer
Forcepoint

> Pursue things that you are uncomfortable with, take risks, and support those around you. Lastly, walk this earth with purpose and become the inspiration that the generation behind us needs. If they can see it, they can be it. Be it for them.
>
> – Myrna Soto

Myrna Soto was born in North Miami and grew up primarily in a blue-collar Cuban exile community named Hialeah in southern Florida. Myrna's father is Cuban, and her mother is Puerto Rican. Myrna is a first-generation college graduate. Myrna was the first person in her family to graduate from college and was blessed to succeed in earning a BA from Florida International University, and a Master of Science degree and an MBA from Nova Southeastern University. There were many obstacles for Myrna on her journey, beginning with her education in a blue-collar public school where most, if not all, of her classmates were Hispanic, and the school did not have a reputation that would draw the attention of universities.

Myrna is proud to say that during her time at Hialeah High School she had the ability to take Honors and AP classes that set the stage for her college acceptance. Twenty-five or more years later, the school has become a significant Ivy League feeder school. Because her family did not have the means to pay for her tuition, Myrna needed to work full time while attending college full time. She also took out student loans to finance her studies. Myrna never once felt that the obstacles couldn't be overcome; however, the need to work full time often compromised her ability to add courses to her semesters. Myrna's timeline to complete her bachelor's degree was a little longer than the normal path but it prepared her for what she was able to accomplish both as a student and professionally. Myrna also firmly believes that her introduction to the business world during her college years provided priceless experience that propelled her to succeed early in her career.

The Latino Digital Divide is a significant issue – accessibility is key to the Hispanic community's ability to advance. It affects everything from education and awareness to commerce and to the ability to share influential insights. While working as an executive at Comcast Corporation, Myrna was extremely proud of her efforts to extend accessibility and provide affordable internet connectivity to underserved communities of color. The program was called Internet Essentials. It was groundbreaking, and Myrna recalls that she felt blessed to be part of advocating for that program. However, so much more remains to be done, including access to devices, educating Hispanic communities on how best to utilize digital platforms, and assisting them to be comfortable about how their data and interactions will be utilized and ultimately protected. Myrna explains that as a long-standing cybersecurity professional, she knew the impact of security and privacy-related initiatives. Without them, the community will not trust their internet connections. However, the engagement of Hispanics is critical to their collective progress. How we get a seat at the table is through our representative leaders, using their influence on the items Myrna mentioned. Myrna also expresses the need to have a voice in the boardrooms of major corporations.

Myrna feels blessed with the fact that she currently serves on three publicly traded boards and uses those opportunities to support community outreach and philanthropy. This includes digital engagement.

There are many ways to promote inclusion, and it starts with making sure people from our community are given the opportunity to pitch their ideas for investment and capital funding opportunities. Myrna also promotes diversity and inclusion whenever she can, as it relates to the development of technology products/services, to ensure that the needs of diverse communities are represented. This can be as simple as accommodating language preferences, or usability testing with a diverse slate of participants, or targeting marketing to appeal to diverse communities. Myrna also promotes inclusion in hiring practices and track record, providing opportunities to diverse candidates who are qualified but need the door opened so they can prosper. Myrna's time as a board member and vice chairperson at HITEC was a very fulfilling time, as her focus was on making sure they had a platform to support more Hispanics in IT Executive roles. After serving for 10 years, Myrna is thrilled to see the mission continue with great success. In the boardroom, Myrna has the opportunity to do the same and represent our community in the boardroom, where she is often the only Latina in the room, but proud to be there to carry the message and mission accordingly. Myrna is a firm believer that if you can see it, you can be it. Myrna is hopeful that she has provided generations behind her to "see it," and has supported the "be it." Myrna states that she won't stop, as there is so much more to do.

Myrna believes we need more impact funds that are dedicated to the Latino community, with a fixed and targeted investment thesis to promote more entrepreneurship within the Latino community. Many of the other diverse populations in the United States have recently seen impact and targeted funds for their respective communities. Latinos need the same. We need a stronger ecosystem of capital access for Latino communities, as well as legal advisors to ensure our community is not taken advantage of in the form of obtuse ownership dilution and matters around operational control. Having funding and losing too much of those items will not promote the success of this population but could potentially exploit them. The barrier to entry needs to be adjusted but the expected protections of the entrepreneur should be maintained.

Myrna always looks for product market fit and the potential exit path for the organization. The exit path may be from a private company to an IPO, a strategic acquisition of the investment into a larger company, or the growth path to exit as an investor and allow the organization to reclaim their cap table after rewarding the investor. There are many great ideas out there, but realistically understanding the product market fit, the demand of the consumer or customer, is critical. A great investor can see the potential and applicability of products or services well ahead of what might exist today. This includes providing the organization guidance to get there.

Myrna has served as a corporate director/board member for seven years. Myrna serves on three publicly traded boards: Consumers Energy (CMS), a member of the Fortune 500; Spirit Airlines (SAVE); and Popular, Inc. (BPOP), which operates as Banco Popular in Puerto Rico and the Virgin Islands, and Popular Bank on the U.S. mainland (New York, New Jersey, and Florida). With the exception of Popular, Myrna has been the only Hispanic board member on two boards, and the only female technology executive.

Myrna believes that Latinos need to be more organized and vocal around the need to have many more representatives on public and private boards. Other diverse communities have gotten more traction and more calls to action of late, and we need to quickly have similar results. Myrna continues to advocate at every opportunity, including mentoring up-and-coming executives, so that they are "board ready," as well as personally recommend board-ready candidates to her colleagues for consideration. However, Latinos as a community need to speak with the power of their pockets and consider not supporting organizations financially who have not taken the appropriate actions to move in the right direction and plan for Hispanic representation in the board room. Our counterparts at LCDA are working very hard on this initiative, and our collective support to represent the caliber of our people is critical. Lastly, we need to have our Hispanic counterparts consider serving on nonprofit and private boards in addition to having the ambition to serve on a public board. This type of experience is extremely valuable when board candidates are evaluated, especially when the candidate may not have Fortune 500–level corporate experience.

Grace Colón
President and CEO
InCarda Therapeutics, Inc.

> Every moment is an organizing opportunity, every person a potential activist, every minute a chance to change the world.
>
> — Dolores Huerta

> A fundamental concern for others in our individual and community lives would go a long way in making the world the better place we so passionately dreamt of.
>
> — Nelson Mandela

Grace Colón grew up in San Juan, Puerto Rico. Her dad's family had been there for generations, and he met her mom, who was from New Orleans, at school in Louisiana (now the University of Louisiana in Lafayette). Her dad studied animal husbandry and worked for decades in the dairy industry in Puerto Rico. He ran one of the largest dairy plants on the island. His dad had studied chemical engineering at Louisiana State University and had worked in the sugar industry in Puerto Rico. Grace's maternal grandfather had studied electrical engineering at Tulane and was involved in building the electrical grid in New Orleans. Therefore, Grace was not a first-generation college graduate, and was fortunate to grow up in a family that was extremely supportive of her early strong interest in science and engineering. Grace was also fortunate to grow up on a beautiful tropical island, surrounded by lush nature on land and sea, which instilled in her a love of life and science and a sense of wonder about our planet.

Grace was fortunate to do well in school and to be accepted at several top engineering schools, but she needed financial aid and worked part time at school and then paid back student loans for many years. Work study had its advantages, though: it enabled her to get a job in research in genetic engineering at the University of Pennsylvania during the mid-1980s, when the field was nascent. This set Grace on a path to obtaining a PhD in chemical engineering at MIT. Grace had the opportunity to participate in a Minority Introduction to Engineering program at MIT when she was a junior in high school, and this allowed her to dream of the possibility of attending there one day.

Grace states, "I had many more opportunities than obstacles." Her family was not wealthy or even well-off by any means, and while she had a quality high school education, she did not have the benefit of AP classes or advanced coursework. That, plus the fact that she had to work many hours to help pay for school, and the cultural differences between Puerto Rico and the Northeast, made her under-graduate years very tough. Grace persisted and did well enough to eventually go to graduate school, but Grace had to work much harder and many more hours than her class-mates just to get middling grades.

Although according to the National Telecommunications and Information Administration, the digital divide for Latinos continues to narrow, in 2017 only 72 percent of Latinos had access to the internet. Latinos still lag behind in terms of access to laptops and broadband com-pared to Caucasians (57 percent vs. 82 percent, and 61 per-cent vs. 79 percent, respectively). However, smartphones have leveled the playing field somewhat, at least in terms of internet access.

The pandemic exacerbated these problems and greatly con-tributed to widening the opportunity gap, as nearly 40 percent of Latinos lacked broadband access at home and 32 percent lacked a computer. Many students resorted to doing their homework in parking lots to access public hotspots.

This situation is unconscionable for all disadvantaged groups. For Latinos in particular, language barriers and immigration concerns amplify these disparities. For this and for so many other reasons, we need to ensure representation and active participation at all levels of government, aca-demia, industry, and nonprofits. Only then will there be true advocacy to address these inequities.

As a long-time executive in a highly technical field, she learned early on that you can't manage what you don't measure. Latinos/Latinx need to be at the table to know even which questions are important to ask, and how best to collect the data to answer them and propose actionable solutions.

At her current company (around 25 employees/part-time consultants), more than half of her employees are either women, people of color, or both. The CEO, the chief medical officer, and the chief operating and technical officer are also of Latino descent. They are extremely conscious of diversity in hiring and make it a priority.

Grace believes in a stereotype, which she states happens to be true: Latinos/Latinx are hardworking, resilient, and believe in working for the good of the community. Grace believes that Latinos are second to none at networking and looking out for each other, because it's part of the culture. Even though Latinos/Latinx come from many, many countries and regions and from subcultures within countries, these values are common to all. Latinos/Latinx will succeed by banding together, raising their voices, and taking action to combat disparities. A great example is the Latino Corporate Directors Association (LCDA), of which Grace is a proud member and supporter. LCDA works tirelessly to champion Latino/Latinx executives, as well as to hold corporations accountable to diversify their boards. They also work closely with other groups championing not only Latino/Latinx causes, but causes related to other under-represented groups.

The main obstacles include the well-established foundation of the current power structures, which is difficult to dismantle, as well as socioeconomic factors that impede educational and career opportunities at every stage. This is why we need to push for representative leadership in all fields, at all levels.

Grace's greatest achievement is that she has become a recognized leader in her field and she contributed to advances in key areas of biotechnology and healthcare. As an executive, serial entrepreneur, and board member of public and private companies, she is passionate about improving patient management and outcomes in chronic diseases, which disproportionately affect under-represented groups, and in particular Latinos. Grace also has been involved in a number of efforts around gender, ethnic, and LGBTQ parity, as well as social entrepreneurship, which she believes is key in bolstering socioeconomic justice globally.

Information is power. This is especially important for the Latino community because, if used properly, connectivity can greatly democratize education, career advancement, healthcare, financial security, and many other factors that enable happy and productive lives.

Grace sits on the board of her own company, InCarda Therapeutics, which is developing breakthrough therapies for atrial fibrillation and other cardiopulmonary conditions. Grace is also an executive chair of ProterixBio, a company developing and commercializing disease management solutions that integrate novel bioclinical analytics with digital tools to improve the effectiveness and efficiency of chronic disease care; the first areas of focus include chronic obstructive pulmonary disease (COPD) and COVID serology testing. Grace also serves on the board of CareDx (CDNA), a leading molecular diagnostics company focused on the discovery, development, and commercialization of clinically differentiated, high-value diagnostic solutions for transplant patients. Previously, Grace served on the boards of PerceptiMed, Paradigm Diagnostics, and Cocoon Biotech.

Grace believes that we can elevate the future by working to increase representation at all levels. Grace is involved in several initiatives to increase representation on boards.

Grace frequently speaks on diversity issues and actively mentors many women and under-represented founders and CEOs of early stage companies.

Ralph de la Vega
Former Vice Chairman
AT&T, Inc.

Don't let anyone put limitations on what you can achieve!

— Ralph de la Vega

Ralph de la Vega was born in Cuba and immigrated to the United States by himself when he was 10 years old. When he arrived, he found himself with a new family, in a new country, without a word of English, and with not a penny in his pockets. So he knows what it means to lose everything and have to start over again.

When he discussed his plans to become an engineer with his high school counselor, the counselor looked at Ralph's grades and his family's financial situation and recommended that he become a mechanic instead. So Ralph dropped out of regular high school to attend a trade school and learn how to be a mechanic. After his grandmother (*abuela*) arrived from Cuba, she told him to ignore the counselor's advice and return to high school and resume his dreams to become an engineer. She said "Ralph, don't let anyone put limits on what you can achieve. If you want to be an engineer you can become an engineer." His *abuela* was a schoolteacher in Cuba and knew the value of an education. Ralph went back to high school then went on to college and earned his engineering degree. The rest is history. Ralph went on to become vice chairman of AT&T, one of the largest corporations in the world, and was the first Hispanic inducted into the U.S. Wireless Hall of Fame.

Ralph believes that the digital divide knows no boundaries: it impacts all ethnicities. Ralph believes that Latinos must continue to find ways to get access to emerging technologies and the internet for young Latino people everywhere. It is not only an essential ingredient for their capability to learn and get an education but also to understand how to navigate the future work environment, which is increasingly digital and mobile.

Ralph promotes diversity and inclusion because diversity and inclusion are good for business and it is also the right thing to do. During his business career, domestically and internationally, he found that inspired, talented, and diverse groups of people deliver outstanding results. In many cases they were able to accomplish what they thought was impossible to achieve.

During his tenure as CEO of AT&T Mobility, his team was able to capture the number-one market share in the postpaid-wireless market for the Hispanic, African American, and Asian segments. They accomplished this by making sure their team had people from those segments leading efforts to market to and service their customers.

The best data Ralph can give to prove this point is that between the period of 2004–2014 his team at Cingular Wireless and AT&T Mobility generated $50 billion in revenues, $23 billion in EBITDA, and won the JD Power Award for the best customer satisfaction in the retail wireless sector.

Ralph believes the key for success in the future for anyone is to get the best education you can get and continue learning your entire life. This also includes working hard and doing your job with the highest degree of integrity.

Ralph believes his greatest achievement is knowing that 23 people who worked directly in his organizations have gone on to become CEOs. Half of those have been women and minorities. He thinks one of the key functions of any executive is not only to deliver great results but also to build a great team that can continue the legacy for the company or business into the future.

Ralph believes that households and the need for connectivity is a necessity, whether a person has a job or is looking for a job in today's environment. The pandemic has demonstrated the need to get everyone connected, and the capability to work from anywhere will be a requirement for successful companies in the future.

Ralph serves on the boards of American Express, New York Life, and Amdocs Corporations. These are Fortune 500 companies with a global reach. Ralph also serves on the boards of Ubicquia and Outreach, two start-up companies that have the capability to become unicorns (reach a $1 billion valuation or more) in the near future.

Lou Sandoval
Chief Executive Officer
SupplyHive

Life can only be understood backwards; but it must be lived forwards.

— *Søren Kierkegaard*

Lou Sandoval grew up on the south side of Chicago in a blue-collar household. He had a working-class upbringing and was the first generation to attend college, like so many other Latino executives today. His background offered Lou a combination of the ability to access educational resources (i.e., he had a home computer to do term papers) and a lack of others to guide him in the process and requirements of how to apply to colleges. As the oldest in his generation, he naturally was the pioneer, the test pilot for the college experience. Lou credits his ability to navigate the inherent obstacles he encountered to the many life mentors and role models, including his parents, who acted as his "little angels," making sure that he succeeded along the way. He states that there is no such thing as being "self-made" because *everyone* needs someone to help guide them. As the first child, he leveraged many opportunities to reduce the steepness in his learning curve.

Lou's paternal grandparents on his dad's side were migrant workers in the Bracero program in the 1930s. They lived in the town of Tanhuato de Guerrero, Michoacán (just outside Morelia) during the winter months, where they were also farmers. His aunts and uncles were born in various western plains states. His father was born in Summit Lake, Minnesota. As an American citizen by birthright, he considered himself one of the original "anchor babies." Later, at the age of 18, he returned to the United States to work in the steel mills of Chicago for 41 years. It is there that Lou's father met his mother. On his mother's side, like many other Mexican immigrants of the 1950s, his grandparents immigrated to Chicago from Mexico City in 1958, seeking economic opportunities (i.e., employment in the steel industry) that our great country provided. They made their home in the neighbor-hood of South Chicago, which is the oldest Mexican American community in the city, dating back to 1908. His mom had a high school education and some vocational school, and his father completed eighth grade and some trade and voca-tional training. His dad gave up his dream of pursuing his education for the economic reality of a job at the United States Steel Mill–South works in Chicago. His mother worked until his brother was born in 1967, after which she stayed home and raised her family. From his parents, he learned the values of hard work, education, and self-improvement in pursuit of his dreams.

His father believed that the single greatest gift he could offer his children was the gift of education. He worked over-time hours in what was considered the great working-class position of a steelworker to provide for them. By living modestly and frugally, Lou's dad was able to put him, his brother, and two younger sisters through 12 years of private education in Catholic schools, at times having to pay tuition for two children at a time.

An additional influence in his educational upbringing was his involvement in Boy Scouts. This had a strong influence and encouraged his desire to pursue a STEM education and become a doctor. En route to obtaining the rank of Eagle Scout, he engaged in every science-based merit badge, which furthered his love for science and technology. His Scout lead-ers and merit badge counselors challenged him to continue his education. The Arias family knew the process of applying for scholarships and was instrumental in helping him get a scholarship from the League of United Latin American Citizens (LULAC) for his leadership in high school and academic performance. The obstacles of educational funding were lessened by the fact that he was a good student in school. He graduated second in his class from grammar school and in the top 5 percent of his high school class. This created the opportunity for a merit-based academic scholarship to DePaul University, where he majored in biochemistry with a minor in physics, psychology, and chemistry. He commuted to school during his freshman year because he could not afford the room and board (which was not covered by the scholarships). His parents still had three other tuitions to pay, which left little extra cash during that time, coupled with the challenging economics of the globalization of the American steel industry. His dad's income was interrupted several times in the 1980s and ultimately ended in 1992, when he was forced to retire early because the steel mill closed. His dad's experience was the same as that of over 16,000 other workers. His neighborhood and the south side of Chicago has never recovered. With the course load of a premed major, commuting was challenging, and Lou's grades suffered a bit during his freshman year. He decided to live on campus and work more hours to pay for room and board. He worked part-time in college as a resident advisor and in other co-op positions in chemistry labs within the private sector to gain experience in his major. Throughout college, he balanced working part-time with his studies to meet his goal of paying for his education.

Lou graduated from DePaul and was accepted to medical school at Loyola University Medical Center. The summer following his college years, he worked at Argonne National Laboratory with his professor from Loyola, who sparked his passion for the pharmaceutical side of the business. With a sudden change of heart and desire to pursue the business side of healthcare, he regretfully informed his parents that he did not want to become a doctor. He withdrew from medical school, one week prior to the start of the year. As luck might have it, he had interviewed with a company named Abbott Laboratories on campus earlier that spring. In the fall of 1988, he received a telegram inviting him to interview for a new program they had started for science students with a strong grade-point average and a track record of leadership experience. In January 1989, he began his career in the pharmaceutical industry with Abbott.

Lou pressed his managers to sponsor him into the leadership program at the company because it would help further his education. As part of their leadership development program, he was supported in continuing his business education at Northwestern University's Kellogg School of Management, where he completed his graduate studies in 2001.

As Lou looks back on his education in the 1970s and 1980s and his blue-collar upbringing, he sees that completing his education was a huge accomplishment. He still remembers the day of his graduation from DePaul. His grandparents and parents were so proud of the first child to graduate from college! As he looks back at the experiences he navigated, he is reminded of the barriers that existed. In the 1980s, something as simple as having access to an electric typewriter to complete term papers was a challenge. He is sure that many of his fellow students did not have the same obstacles, as he would hear about how they had typewriters and word processors at home. The closest he would come to these tools in high school was going to the public library and waiting in line to jump on a DOS-based PC with his 5¼-inch floppy disk to type out a term paper. His family would also borrow an electric typewriter from a well-respected community member, known as Mr. Arias, when his children were not using it.

Cities like Chicago that have existed on the premise of segregation magnify inequalities among populations. Within two miles of the thriving tech corridor of the West loop – which is home to such companies as Google, Fourkites, Otis, and Transunion – are some of the most underserved Black and Brown communities in the city. It is incumbent on Hispanics in leadership positions to make companies aware of this and the need to socially impact these communities, if not from a perspective of "the right thing to do," then in order to create an economic impact that will lead to long-term workforce development opportunities for Latino students who want to pursue careers in technology. As the largest minority group in the city, and soon to be the majority population, Latinos/Latinx are the tech company's workforce of the future.

Creating foundational change in bridging the technical divide will require that Hispanics leverage their collective leadership voice to make sure that companies of all verticals take notice and invest in our communities. This will be even more important in the post–pandemic period as digital transformation will come to the forefront. In this transformation, there will be a loss of some jobs, which will be replaced by technology. Many tech professionals knew that these transformations were coming; the pandemic just accelerated them. If Latinos/Latinx are not offered a seat at the decision-making table, then they should make their own. Not creating equity is tantamount to impeding economic growth in all Hispanic communities. Latinos/Latinx must insist on the funding of public-private partnerships that help fund development of coding skills in K–12 education. The creation of tech incubators and partnership with angel investors that help fund start-ups will help foster what the Latino community does best, to unfold entrepreneurial talents.

Lou's company leverages a software platform, which helps measure one of the major drivers that companies use to define the impact of their diversity, equity, and inclusion initiatives – supplier diversity development and procurement. Supplier diversity development in its basic forms is one that Lou was raised with. His understanding is that "to whom much is given, much is expected in return." Lou has been blessed in his career to have overcome some big challenges to get to where he is today. In doing so, he has never forgotten his roots. His high school mascot was the pioneer. Fittingly, because throughout his life he had many "firsts," Lou sees it as his responsibility to help more people to "climb the ladder." In his role on the board of Wintrust bank, he was the first nonwhite board member in the history of the bank. When he joined six years ago, he asked senior management for the commitment that in one year, the diversity of their board would increase to 33 percent and in four years it would be 40 percent or greater. In December 2020, they reached the milestone of 50 percent diversity by gender and equal diversity by ethnicity (i.e., Black, white, Latino, etc.). Lou accomplished this by becoming involved in the nominating, compensation, and governance committee. He has taken an active hand in the deliverables sector.

Lou has fought to ensure diversity in the boating industry, as well. His pathway to boating is an atypical one. He did not grow up sailing or in a yacht club. For him, it all started with an invitation to participate in Boy Scouts, which led to sailing during summer camp. He raised money to attend the camp by selling chocolates, because summer camps were expensive for a family with four Catholic school tuitions to pay. Later in life he would return to sailing in his professional career when he was invited to participate with colleagues at Abbott. This led to reviving his love of the sport.

Lou's career would take him to Seattle and Miami, where he had the opportunity to compete in races from Los Angeles to Honolulu and from Newport to Bermuda, primarily on other people's boats. It was not until he returned to Chicago that he was able to buy his own boat, which led to the opportunity to sail on Lake Michigan and eventually led to his purchase of the dealership that sold him the boat – the path least traveled, one might say. He pursued his dream of business ownership, which led to prominence and notoriety in the marine industry and thrust him into the role of being a spokesperson for diversifying the sport and the industry. This is a role that he has taken on for the past 15 years and as an active racing sailor – he still lives it.

Lou is the first nonwhite commodore in 145 years of Chicago Yacht Club's history. Lou never expected that his two-year term would result in having to lead the club through the pandemic. There is no preparation for that occurring, much like having to take command of a vessel. Lou mentions they had sought to break down the measurables for the year – navigating uncertainty and overcoming the intangibles of business shutdowns, creating a safe environment for their employees and their members.

His vision as CEO of SupplyHive is to grow the company into becoming a $100 million company in two years. One might say those are steep goals, but he will accomplish it through principle-centered leadership and applying what he has learned in navigating over 30,000 miles at sea. Lou is a deeply passionate founder who has created a company, and the board has brought him on to navigate the growth of the company because of his background as an entrepreneurial builder of businesses, brands, and high-performing teams. They will leverage the growth of the company by keeping true to the principles of creating value for the investors, shareholders, employees, and the communities in which they live and work. They will do so with transparency, accountability, and equity. They will do it the Latino way.

2

Intelligence
Healthcare and Physicians

José Raul Bolaños, MD
CEO and Founder
Nimbus-T Global

I would say, use your brain to excel at what is in your heart and find success!

— José Bolaños

JOSÉ RAUL BOLAÑOS IS THE oldest of seven children. He was born in Aldea Bolaños in El Salvador. His family moved to Los Angeles when he was three years old. José went to public schools up through high school and began excelling in the fifth grade. He was very excited about math, science, woodworking, and cars.

José scored the highest in the country in the Armed Forces Battery Test and was offered a position at West Point. Because he had no one to give him advice on making this decision, José waited and was ultimately accepted to the University of Southern California (USC) and UC Berkeley. José got a scholarship to USC and went there. He feels blessed with the ability to use his brain and intelligence and went on to major in biomedical engineering. Later, he transferred to the University of California at Irvine to major in biology (BS). Subsequently he went to UC Davis Medical School and ultimately to Stanford and finished as an ob/gyn and fertility specialist. José was in private medical practice for 22 years and delivered over 5,000 babies. "God has been good," is how José describes his life.

He began his medical practice in Los Gatos, California (mid-upper income) and subsequently purchased a medical practice in East San José that allowed him to care for more Latino patients. He created his own information system, medical records, labs, and billing system. One problem arose: José had 10,000 patient records. When planning to transfer the records into the electronic medical record, he learned that the identifying numbers were 12 to 16 digits, which did not allow for his thousands of patients. José created an algorithm that created a unique ID for every one of the patients: "first name initial+last name" – and eight digits for the birthdate. Problem solved, and that was about 25 years ago!

After taking care of the Latino community in East San José, it became clear to José that there was a need for more Latino doctors. José has always felt it to be important to be a role model for younger doctors, because only 5.8 percent of U.S. physicians are Hispanic. He realized that the number of physicians documented by the Association of American

Medical Colleges shows that more millennials and generation Z Latino students need to focus on their educational aspirations to become physicians, especially after experiencing the disparities of Latinos impacted by COVID-19.

José's efforts have been to continue to solve problems in electronic records and cybersecurity. He is also concerned that most enterprise systems lack security. Today, over 10 billion usernames and passwords are compromised and on the dark web! Criminals are stealing over one third of $3.5 trillion in healthcare expenditures. The United States is struggling with problems caused by the COVID-19 pandemic, as many workers are working from home and logging in with their passwords and posing a massive cybersecurity risk. José is the CEO of a two-year-old start-up that has a patent on a new identity and login process (with no passwords). José states that they have an app that is used to login to a new splash screen on your computer that reads your Dynamic Nimbus-Key ID (encrypted QR code) and a dynamic PIN. This protects the enterprise with a revolutionary new cybersecurity front door lock.

When José was a teenager, they all worked for his dad, who had his own woodworking shop. His dad taught him how to be his own boss. When you are your own boss, you control your destiny. What José has seen in inequities in our society is very interesting. Employed Latinos have all been underpaid and abused in many instances and without recourse, resulting in an unjust society. Others who have made carts to sell food or who have built their own businesses have been more successful!

Arturo Loaiza-Bonilla, MD
Vice Chairman of the Department of Medical Oncology
Cancer Treatment Centers of America

Our fate, whatever it be, is to be overcome by our patience under it. Fortune favors the brave.

— Virgil

Arturo Loaiza-Bonilla was born and raised in Bogotá, Colombia. His parents were separated early in his life and he was raised by his hardworking mother, who, as the eldest of nine children, managed to pursue a master's degree and provide him a dignified life and strong values of grit, resilience, and appreciation for the small things in life. He experienced his maternal grandfather's death from end-stage renal disease due to lack of appropriate medical care when he was a teenager and resolved to become the first physician in his family. His grandfather told him that he believed in him and was hopeful and proud of his grandson having achieved what many other believed impossible at the age of 16. He died shortly after this encouraging talk.

Medical school in Colombia is quite expensive, and Arturo's best chance was to be accepted to the National University of Colombia, which is public, but also quite hard to get into: less than 1 percent of applicants are admitted after a single national ranked exam; few thought he would make it.

As he advanced in his education, Arturo became passionate about genomics and research, and decided to pursue the

American dream. He started buying all of his medical school books in English, which were much cheaper and up-to-date, and borrowed over 5,000 pages of second-hand photocopies of preparation books for the U.S. Medical Licensing Examination, while downloading another book using a now-defunct peer-to-peer file-sharing application, called Kazaa. He took a job as a website developer for his medical school, and saved the scholarship money awarded to him as one of the top two students of his class so that he could pay for the first test to make his dream come true.

After completing medical school, he worked three jobs, averaging 100 hours per week for about two years while studying for the U.S. boards. Arturo landed in Baltimore with no credit history or family support to start his residency in internal medicine. This was a journey that would take him to the National Institutes of Health, Johns Hopkins University, the University of Miami, and the University of Pennsylvania.

As a second-generation college graduate and physician in his research leadership role, he was hopeful that his daughter Natalia would share his common passion for education and betterment of their lives through dedication, emotional intelligence, and smart work. This is the care of the evolution of Latino digital intelligence.

Arturo believes academic institutions, starting from early public education, should continue to realize the importance of technology and digital solutions to improve access to knowledge and to involve their end users in the development of those tools. Many initiatives in digital health, including those focused on helping Spanish-speaking folks, are envisioned, and developed in innovation environments like

Silicon Valley. They look great in PowerPoint, but no one uses them, and millions of dollars go to waste. This is because Latinos did not have a seat at the design table.

The first step to overcome this gap between innovation and reality is that Latinos must lose our fear of trying something outside of the box. Be bold and take chances beyond your comfort zone. We need to create an entrepreneurial environment inclusive of Latinx. We must be part of incubators, and include a diverse mindset for founders, workers, and end users.

This is also true if Latinos are not to be left behind in the digital health revolution. Latinos are affected by advanced stages of cancer more often than the general population, mostly due to lack of access to screening and healthcare, and because of cultural issues. Many times, we are concerned about sharing the diagnosis with other family members, lack access to genetic counseling, and defer talking to our primary physicians when we could have detected the cancer at a curable stage. That is why Cancer Treatment Centers of America created a national campaign, called "No Esperes" in collaboration with the National Hispanic Medical Association and the U.S. Hispanic Chamber of Commerce, in which they aim to educate, empower, and promote a culture of early detection for Hispanic patients and family members. They demystify screening, use resources that are culturally congruent, and get folks excited about nascent technologies that use advanced imaging and liquid biopsies.

While working in academia, Arturo realized how difficult it was for cancer patients to access care in a prompt fashion, including clinical trials, and how AI, digital tools, and innovative approaches may help to bridge that gap between the Latino/Latinx community, academics, precision medicine, and social determinants of health. Given that personal experience, Arturo decided to become an entrepreneur and cofounded Massive Bio, with the vision to accelerate cancer research and inspire others to do the same in their respective fields.

Fortunately, many academic institutions and medical schools are identifying the need for a diverse class of medical students, inclusive of women and different backgrounds, such as Latinx, and African Americans. The best way to promote this inclusion effort is to praise it, highlight it, and for Latinos to excel at these opportunities, once given. Many times, it is fear of being rejected, giving up before trying, or a sense of entitlement that leads promising and likely successful applicants to think they cannot pursue their dream of becoming a physician. Arturo mentions that it imperative for the Latino community to continue being our own best advocates and empower those interested in STEM careers.

Once we identify those leaders and share their stories, we can inspire future generations to pursue their dreams. Arturo mentions that he sees this in his own family, where younger members are already in medical school or working to reach leadership roles. They are paving the way and leading by example.

Since his early years of medical training, Arturo has learned the importance of mentorship and collaboration with younger generations. At every level, from residency, post-doctorate fellowship, faculty member, medical leader, and digital health biotechnology entrepreneur, he strived to find and sponsor promising individuals, looking to create a positive impact on our society. We need to continue creating local, regional, and nationwide networks to foster those relationships. It does not have to be that hard; Arturo emphasizes how we are all in this together, and our legacy will live on in those whom we help. That sense of cooperation is what led to our success as a species and to overcome war, famine, pandemics, and global challenges. The sky is the limit if we all work together with a common purpose and goal.

As a parent, he empathizes with the difficulties of working parents and understands the challenges of our proactive involvement in our children's education, particularly in a society that rewards individualistic behavior but has a short memory of previous challenges. The Hispanic culture is always centered around family values, collaboration, and traditions, and we need to strongly instill these beliefs in our future generations. We respect and care about our elders, we are not afraid of expressing our feelings and opinions or helping our family members in times of need, and we love to tell stories. That sense of belonging, collaboration, and shared values around our bilingual families shall be the cornerstone that keeps our children open to asking for our opinions, learning from our past errors, and capitalizing on our successes. Telling them stories of prior generations overcoming challenges they faced and encouraging them to be good citizens, love and respect themselves and others, and contribute to their own lives and society will keep them engaged and realize it is not merely good fortune, but grit, dedication, empathy, persuasion, passion for what we do, and ambition to better ourselves that bring real success.

Federico W. von Son de Fernex, MD
CEO
Somos, Inc.

"Build your wings on the way down."
This is my everyday mantra. I truly think that you can never be
READY enough to actually start something. You just have to go
for it and fix whatever needs to be fixed during the process.
— Federico W. von Son de Fernex

Federico W. von Son de Fernex was born in Baja, California, and raised in Cuernavaca, a beautiful small town in the central region of México, euphonism of the Nahuatl word "Cuauhnāhuac," which means "near the woods or surrounded by trees" (it was known as the city of the eternal spring, thanks to Alexander von Humboldt). Federico considered himself a global citizen. A young soccer athlete, he was fortunate to experience the huge contrast of living in one of the most organized and well-structured countries, like Switzerland, and also its counterparts, like Argentina and México. After more than 11 years as a semi-pro and pro soccer player, his decision to study medicine became very clear.

His father graduated from medical school in the 1970s and pioneered the noninvasive aesthetics field in Latin America for more than 20 years before he passed away in 2019. His grand- and great-grandfathers (maternal lineage) were both renowned and successful urology surgeons, one of them the founder and the other ex-president of the Mexican Society of Urology in the 1950s. Even with that illustrious medical lineage, Frederico never received any guidance from his father on how to make the best out of medical school (his father was very hermetic, as he was raised by a military veteran and both parents lived through civil and world wars, so feelings and bonding weren't allowed). Federico had to do the research myself, find out which universities were the top ranked in México, and determine his options after finishing his medical training. At that point, he didn't know that his paternal grandfather had started some engineering studies at MIT and that he could follow in his footsteps or continue his studies in the United States or Europe.

As a medical doctor, he realized that diversity in scientific research, drug development, therapeutics, and prevention strategies is crucial to understand and treat Mexican and Latino patients more accurately; yet, Latinos and African Americans together represent less than 4 percent of the names in available databases.

Scientific institutions and researchers have an old-fashioned mindset, where data gatekeeping is a standard and decentralization seems to be a sweet dream.

Actually, Federico has found the perfect name for them: Scientificsaurus (from the Latin word *scientia*, meaning "knowledge," and *saurus*, meaning more commonly "dinosaur").

This is a common scenario that we face every day in Latin American countries, and you can fight against it only with disruptive and inclusive thinking. Again, inclusion and coparticipation is the way to go, and if we want to understand Latinos better, we need to invite them to play the same game; no one can be left out. As a personal mission, which he feels grateful to share with his cofounder, friend, and one of the smartest people he has ever known, they decided to invite

Indigenous Nations, communities, and leaders to participate in transparent and decentralized data aggregation.

This might sound very trite for Latinos immersed in entrepreneurship within the United States, but the real barrier starts with venture capital firms and angel investors. It takes three to four times longer for Latinos to raise capital than other groups (around one year to 18 months). According to a Crunchbase analysis from the past five years, only around 2.4 percent of total funding was allocated to Latino founders. The key for success relies on becoming *very* proactive (three to four times more than the average non-Latino entrepreneur – statistics don't lie and Dr. Federico mentions that we need to counteract this imbalance), resilient, and to create a network of great Latinos that have already gone through the same situation. That could help in structuring important partnerships and alliances or doing warm introductions to investors and funds (use the digital tools, i.e., LinkedIn, to connect and prosper).

In Europe, they love the hard work, passion, and extreme ability they acquire in Mexico and Latin America, thanks to the high number of patients we fortunately interact with. In the end, he was accepted in the second-ranked hospital in Helvetia at that time. The story tells itself, here is how Federico's road to success in entrepreneurship began . . . Yes, after all that effort, rejections, and long nights, he decided to drop out from the residency program that cost him years of sacrifice to help millions of people by innovating in healthcare. In the end, you have to follow your dream no matter what it takes, and even if you encounter hundreds of uphill battles, you need to listen to your heart and fight for it.

Irene Chavez
Senior Vice President and Area Manager
Kaiser Permanente

There is no failing – there is only learning.

– Irene Chavez

Irene Chavez grew up in the rural area of San Elizario, Texas, up until the age of 12. Irene's grandfather entered the United States through the Bracero program, and her dad was six years old. Thereafter, she grew up in El Paso, Texas. Irene is the fourth of eight children – six boys and two girls. Irene's father did not attend schools; instead he was self-taught: English, grammar, and math. Irene's father had a curiosity for picking up a book and studying the subject matter on his own. Her father served in the U.S. Army during World War II and retired from the U.S. Customs service, now known as ICE. He earned a Purple Heart, which they learned about only after he died. Her father was strict, easy to anger, and often physically abusive toward all of them. Irene's mom was from Parral, Chihuahua, Mexico, and married her father, who was 14 years older. She was a homemaker and learned to cope with her difficulties in interesting ways, teaching and modeling the value of finding joy despite the situation one lives in.

Irene was the first to graduate with a university bachelor's degree and the only one to secure a masters level degree. Irene's father did not believe a girl should go to college, providing no support or encouragement. Irene's mom, on the other hand, was her inspiration, with the mantra of "Education will ensure independence from financial struggles, a controlling and abusive situation, and will offer opportunities to contribute to a better quality of life." Irene graduated from a girl's parochial school as the valedictorian. She worked full time to pay the tuition at the University of Texas at El Paso. Irene graduated with a liberal arts bachelor's degree in political science with a minor in secondary education. Her goal was to teach American history and American government.

Irene worked with Providence Memorial Hospital as a night clerk to earn the tuition money. Little did Irene know that she would fall in love with healthcare. The digital divide in the Latinx communities underscores the reality of those who have and those who have not.

Access to high-speed internet/network services and a device, be it a computer or smart device, is a nicety – not a "need" – for those earning only a living wage or even less. Irene's experience in El Paso, Texas, was to see the schools, churches, libraries, and Latinx community-based organizations rally to extend high-speed internet and computer/smart device workrooms and/or devices to Latinx communities.

Irene's experience in San José is limited and she may not be fully aware of all the efforts in place to shrink the digital divide. Her expectation is that given the presence of Silicon Valley Giants and a progressive city and county government, that high-speed internet is readily available throughout Santa Clara County. Irene would also expect every Latinx student from elementary school through high school to have access to a computer and or smart devices. If the assessment indicates this is not the current state, she would support starting a campaign to accomplish these goals.

Irene chose healthcare management and then administration because she wanted to make a positive difference in the lives of people who need healthcare services, especially in the Latinx community, with educational resources for diabetes, hypertension, and other factors that have impacted our community. Irene wants to be a role model so that no matter what is in your past, only you control your future. Irene wants to be a role model overcoming fear and to fight the attitude of *aguantate* – "hold on, put up with it, and/or settle."

Irene was inspired to have a purpose and to make a positive difference for her community, most of which was Latinx. She was inspired to make a positive difference for women's health, for the elderly, and most especially for children.

The negative health outcomes caused by the lack of access to healthcare include loss of sight, loss of digits and/or limbs, and the need for dialysis, all because of uncontrolled diabetes. Newborns might receive a diagnosis of "Failure to thrive" caused by a lack of formula. Worst is the abuse of elders and children due to alcoholism, drug abuse, or anger fueled by desperation.

Irene witnessed the abuse of health insurance policies by healthcare providers who would overtreat and/or misdiagnose people to secure more money. The many women labeled psychiatrically ill by male physicians who failed to understand menopause and/or family abuse. Irene witnessed the erosion of trust in the healthcare system, because of the communication gap, resulting in the beliefs held by the Hispanic community.

Irene mentions the fear of many Latinx folks visiting the doctor, because of the beliefs that "She/he will find something wrong with me," or they won't go because "All they want is just to get money" or "Why go? They don't listen anyway."

To change the narrative:

- Begin to educate in kindergarten – teach good health habits and continue the education through high school. Invest in prevention!
- Enter social contracts with famous people from sports, music, acting, and so forth to leverage their status with positive messaging and support for their communities.
- Get involved in the community. Invest in your community. Hire from your community. Promote from your community.

Face your fear and overcome it; take the risk and make the decision. Stay hungry to learn, and seek input from interesting people by asking provocative questions. Take on the most difficult job duties, become an expert and indispensable, and be present and in the room. To be noticed one must be a subject matter expert: trusted, reliable, and courageous. When Irene mentors, she loves seeing when a mentee blossoms to their full untapped potential because they believe they have been given permission to do so.

Digital health is inevitable because our youth will demand this level of medical care. Medical care is expected to be in the palm of their hand, in their home, on their refrigerator, in their bathroom, on every appliance, and so on.

With Medicare and Medicaid representing nearly half of any major counties' coverage, the demand to provide a digital/virtual experience is on us. Insurance carriers see the value of providing this level of access to their insureds for various reasons: marketability and ultimately to improve the delivery of medical care. Access to this augmented level of care has so many benefits and yet it is not without risk. Protecting your personal private healthcare information must be ensured by these systems.

Examples of the digital medical tools of the future include smart implanted devices, insulin pumps, heart stents, joint implants, orthotics, and prosthetics; smart pills designed for one's specific illness; smart GI pills to identify lesions within the intestine; smart applications to measure carbs, sugar, protein, fat, and vitamin intake; nanotech medications and inserts, and more.

The future in medicine is all about digital, and it's exciting!

Harold Fernandez, MD
Chief Cardiovascular Surgery
Southside Hospital

All you need is Love.

– The Beatles

Harold Fernandez grew up in Medellin, Colombia, and lived with his grandmothers because his parents were in America working as undocumented immigrants. At the age of 13, not finding a way to bring them legally to the United States, his parents made the difficult decision to smuggle him and his younger brother into America to join them. At the age of 13, he found himself on a tiny Island in the Bahamas (Bimini) waiting for a boat to pick up him, his brother, and 10 other undocumented immigrants. They waited for two weeks on this island for the weather on the ocean to improve.

Finally, on October 26, 1978, they all climbed into a small boat and made the seven-hour trip across a corner of the Bermuda Triangle on the way to the coast of Miami. They left at midnight to avoid being detected by the American Coast Guard. Although they all thought that they would lose their lives, they made it to safety. They then caught a flight to New York and reunited with his parents to start their life in America as undocumented immigrants.

His undocumented status was his greatest obstacle to even applying to college. Harold didn't have legal documents to get into college. He was fortunate to have the support of many compassionate Americans who supported his application to get legal residency, including letters from the New Jersey senator, Bill Bradley, the New Jersey governor, Thomas Kean, and the president of the United States, Ronald Reagan. After many struggles, he was able to get his legal residency and concentrate on working hard to get accepted to Princeton University and then Harvard Medical School. Harold is the first one in his family to graduate from high school and attend college.

In all aspects of our universe, it is obvious that the way we process, generate, and adapt to information is an important factor in how our Latinx community competes in the digital world. As we incorporate our community into this new paradigm, it is important that we do not forget our roots. Harold is a strong advocate for the idea that what makes us unique is also what makes us stand out. Harold explains that this is also what makes us strong. There are, of course, many things that are unique to our cultural heritage within the Latinx community, including our food, our family values, our traditions, and the most important one, in his opinion, is our language. We should continue to emphasize that, as we become more immersed in our beautiful American traditions, including all the digital developments, we do not forget that all the digital information and content is also made available in Spanish. This includes our medical education, delivery of information, and communication with our patients, both in-person and through all digital formats. This is why Harold has worked on his own YouTube channel, *El Show del Doctor Fernandez: Su Salud en Español*. It is designed to inform the LatinX community about their health in Spanish and in a way that they can understand.

One of his most important activities outside the hospital is Harold's participation in his community outreach program that Northwell organizes in New York.

Harold gives a lecture titled "From Immigrant to Cardiac Surgeon." In it, Harold shares his own story of coming to America at the age of 13 and overcoming many obstacles, including having to learn a new language, not having documents, economic struggles, discrimination from other students who would yell at him in the halls to "go back to your own country," and not having anyone in his family who went to high school, let alone college.

But, Harold had one advantage, and at that time he didn't even know it. This was that his grandmothers had instilled in him a strong belief that with hard work everything is possible. So, when he speaks to the young students, he tells them that his story is not just his story, but it is also their story and that of their parents. He reminds them that it is important for them to believe in themselves, and he shares a quote from

Oprah Winfrey: "In life you become not who you want to become, but you become, who you believe you can become." He reminds them that when he started believing in himself, his life changed, and he was able to become a much better student. Many students in Gen Z do not believe that a career in medicine is for them because they don't believe that they can handle the academic rigors of a medical school education. Harold thinks it is important for all of us in leadership positions to do everything we can to share our story and reach out to them through all available digital platforms so they can start to believe in themselves and understand that with hard work all their dreams are possible.

There is nothing more reassuring to an ill patient in a hospital then when a doctor walks into the room and speaks to that patient in their native language. In fact, it is not just a cultural or emotional connection that forms between the patient and the doctor, but there is a lot of evidence that those patients heal better and that the results in terms of care are much better for those patients. As a Latino community, we need to demand that our elected officials and community leaders understand the power and significance of cultural diversity at every level of our society, including universities and professional schools. There is absolutely no excuse for any academic institution to fail at meeting those diversity guidelines that adequately represent our communities. In medicine and in many other industries, the results clearly show that diversity makes us stronger and is the best way to move forward.

So what are best strategies to get parents, especially Spanish-speaking parents, involved in their child's education and helping them to focus on higher education, like medical school?

First, it should not come as a surprise to anyone that knowing two languages will only make you stronger. Both of his kids were born in America, but they learned Spanish at home as their first language. Once they started school, they both learned English quickly and without any delay in their academic progress. Many studies have shown that young kids can learn multiple languages very well at an early age. This will help them in school, in the workplace, and in the digital world as they become immersed in creating content. All parents should play an active role in encouraging their kids and teaching them to be proficient in both reading and writing Spanish.

Second, he feels strongly that parents who are involved in a child's primary education will be parents who are also involved in their kids' higher education. This has to start early. In fact, it has to start by the parent forming a relationship with their kids around a book and learning how to read. This was the goal of Harold's latest book, *A Boy and a Book: Overcoming Obstacles Through the Magic of Reading* (2020). The first story that Harold shares is about sitting with his mother on a sofa reading a book together. This is the most important lesson for us as parents. Teach your kids how to read, teach them how to do it well, and share with them ways in which they may fall in love with reading. This simple, but powerful skill will last with them for all of their life, and will help them greatly during higher education, including medical school.

Harold had the privilege and honor to help thousands of his patients by doing open heart surgery. "This involves getting into the chest of my patients, stopping their hearts, and fixing the arteries and the valves that are not working." Harold is very proud and fortunate to have had some of the best results over the past 20 years in the state of New York. But one of his greatest accomplishments in medicine is yet to come, and it involves a much less invasive way of helping his patients. Over the past five years Harold has discovered the power of preventing and healing chronic diseases through nutrition. Harold is currently a strong proponent of whole food, plant-based nutrition as the best way to prevent and reverse disease, especially cardiovascular disease. Harold has adopted this form of nutrition for himself and his family with excellent results and is very excited and energized to bring this message to his patients, and our Latinx community. He feels strongly that the high levels of obesity, diabetes, high blood pressure, and heart disease are alarming, especially in the Hispanic community and all these conditions can be prevented and reversed if we adopt a plant-based diet. In fact, the high level of these chronic conditions in our community is one of the reasons why we have had such a high mortality during the COVID-19 pandemic. He is currently working on a book and on other digital platforms such as Facebook, YouTube, and Instagram to reach patients with this information. Harold plans to present his ideas in both Spanish and English.

Sergio Aguilar-Gaxiola, MD, PhD
Professor of Clinical Internal Medicine
University of California, Davis School of Medicine

Improving health-care access to quality care for all in need is a collective responsibility issue. Disparities challenge our core values of justice, fairness, and equity. We are morally and socially responsible for improving the disparities in health care because a healthy society is the foundation on which we build our schools, our neighborhoods, and our economy. I know we have a long road to travel in order to achieve equity in access and quality of care. And I am hopeful that perhaps more people than ever are finally waking up to this reality and getting ready to face and solve the challenges.

– Sergio Aguilar-Gaxiola

Sergio Aguilar-Gaxiola believes that this is a unique time in our nation's history. The converging of two historic events, the COVID-19 pandemic and systemic structural racism, are disproportionally impacting underserved communities, and if left unaddressed, the negative consequences can be long lasting. These two incidents have emerged with tremendous force and call on us to take action and achieve transformation. From a health perspective, we are witnessing a devastating impact on both our physical and mental health as a result of the coronavirus pandemic and social isolation. We are also seeing the manifestation of structural racism and differential treatment of our vulnerable communities such as farmworkers, and that has been very concerning and sobering. The demonstrations in response to the preventable killing of George Floyd created a historic mobilization of people from all walks of life—different ages, race and ethnic backgrounds, and sexual orientation and gender identity (SOGI)—a formidable movement elevating justice, equity, diversity, inclusion, and transformation. He remains inspired by the growing solidarity in addressing social injustice. What's been inspiring amid these two historic life-changing events is that we've seen signs of positive change: We have seen the Supreme Court's rulings in favor of LGBTQ rights in the workplace, the protections for DACA students, and the broader reaching out of the UC System relative to affirmative action. These are extraordinary accomplishments, and we cannot help but link these rulings to the effects of the national demonstrations. What has emerged is something we have known for a long time, and that is the differential treatment of humans based on physical characteristics such as color, race, ethnicity, and SOGI. *This just cannot continue to persist.*

Equity is about fairness. For example, community members that need access to care may not have the necessary transportation to get to the services they need when they need them, or maybe they wish to receive services in their preferred language, or they need to be seen at different hours that align with their arduous employment schedules. Equality is about sameness – same solutions across the board, one size fits all. To effectively address disparities, we need fairness. We need to tailor solutions to the unique cultural and language needs of specific populations – it's not a matter of receiving more or less, it is about recognizing what matters most to underserved communities.

The fact is that disparities in access to care and service utilization lead to negative health consequences and ultimately a suboptimal quality of life. For this reason, we must be compelled to provide the best quality of care possible for everyone. Disparities are bad for health policy. Health policy helps us correct the misallocation of resources to the people who need them the least and who derive the least benefit. The 2002 Institute of Medicine landmark report titled "Unequal Treatment: Confronting Racial and Ethnic Disparities in Health Care" introduced evidence in an unequivocal way that created a national debate on unequal treatment for underserved populations; it highlighted research that showed substantial ethnic and racial variation in quality of care. This brought disparities to the attention of the nation and showed that they exist across services and clinical settings. Health equity is a broad topic – we can look at it through language spoken, proxy measures for socioeconomic status, race/ethnicity/SOGI, and even the neighborhoods we live in.

There are many dimensions to equity. The most notable factors are place of birth and immigration status, the place and type of employment, economic and housing stability, and food security. All these factors have played a key role on the disproportionate negative impact on COVID-19-related excess mortality on Latinos, African American, Native American, and other underserved populations. COVID-19 health inequities have become a huge public health challenge, as are inequities in the distribution and uptake of vaccines, particularly by those who are most impacted. We are in dire need of (1) better data that help us drive more equitable decisions in the current COVID-19 response, (2) community-driven solutions to pervasive and systemic COVID-19 inequities, and (3) better preparation for long COVID.

Mario Anglada
CEO
HoyHealth

One step at a time gets the marathon done.

– Mario Anglada

Mario Anglada was born in San Juan, Puerto Rico, to a working-class family. He studied in the public school system and was selected to attend a specialized math and science high school, which led to acceptance to the University of Puerto Rico upon graduation. After arriving in college and studying for two years, Mario decided that he was not ready to determine what his career path would be. He enlisted in the U.S. Army to give himself some time to decide on a future career. Mario spent five years in the U.S. Army, during which he was stationed in Germany and deployed to various conflict areas during his time in service. At the end of his service, Mario returned to Puerto Rico with his family, where he decided to focus his career on the field of business and enrolled in college at night while working full-time for Procter & Gamble. During a five-year period, he was able to earn a double major in business and management and human resources, and continue to earn an MBA in Global Management. After graduation, Mario remained in the business of healthcare with national and international positions at Johnson & Johnson, GF Health, Nestlé Health Science, and Univision Communications before founding Hoy Health.

The Latino community are avid users of technology and use the tools available to them as enablers of their content creation, usually from an artistic perspective in business or from a consumer perspective as end users. Mario believes that, as a community, Latinos haven't had the ability to see ourselves as builders of these tools, and he sees this as the key area for engagement for academia and other stakeholders, by allowing our younger generations to see themselves as the engineers, programmers, and technologists who are creators of the tools. This can be achieved by providing programs to young students, supporting them in a guided manner through their education, and providing a path that encourages appropriate risk-taking to give them a glimpse of the opportunity of creating our own path with a start-up or other entities that aren't necessarily the first choice for many who are culturally conditioned to take a more "traditional" steady, safe path to employment.

Mario's company, Hoy Health, was designed to address the needs of healthcare consumers at the base of the social pyramid, so his products are built to be accessible and affordable by design. Their mission is to ensure that everyone, everywhere, has access to healthcare, regardless of their economic status. Hoy Health has created an ecosystem approach to building their company, ensuring that their consumers have access to bilingual healthcare professionals at all times; access to low-cost medications across the United States, Central/South America, and the Caribbean; and complete chronic condition support solutions that are all-inclusive, offering a simple-to-follow guided path to better manage their health. During the pandemic they have partnered with leading organizations in the healthcare and technology space to make their solutions a tool for these partners to deploy to their member base. These could be a patient who is assisted in monitoring his or her health results at home or a medical practice that uses our solutions to digitize their offerings to provide telemedicine to their patients.

The Latino community should encourage the adoption of new models of care that allow healthcare providers to engage with patients, wherever the patient might be. Taking into account that under 6 percent of medical professionals are of Hispanic origin and 18 percent of the population is of Hispanic origin, we feel that technology can serve as a force multiplier, allowing our community to leverage technology to assist in supporting healthcare professionals to virtual monitor patients, making their outreach to the Latino community more effective in terms of cost, access, and ease of use. One important factor to consider is to allow the creation of a national provider license certification across all 50 states that allows medical providers to provide care across state lines. This approach would allow areas with enough providers to use technology to reach patients in areas that might lack culturally and linguistically appropriate care by providers who speak the language and understand the culture.

The Latino community has a strong emphasis in achieving the collective benefit for the family nuclear group. As such, providers who encourage cross-family education and accountability for care will achieve better health outcomes in their patient populations. This can be as simple as including the larger group in healthcare education to enable them to learn to better support their loved one and their condition to actively encouraging group behavior change to enhance the overall health status of the family group.

Hoy Health has been built to solve the friction points of each healthcare stakeholder. This includes the healthcare provider, the patient, the family, health systems, employers, and the government. In order to support the goals of various stakeholders, they had to design the process as continuous from the start to the end of the patient journey. A big problem with the current healthcare system is the fragmentation that naturally occurs by having each party in their own silo. Having a complete solution allows them to gain stakeholder adoptions from their preferred need that can be met by increasing access, decreasing cost, simplifying complexity, or guiding someone through the complete journey.

Oscar Cervantes, PhD
Assistant Clinical Professor
University of California, San Francisco Medical School

No se rajen y echenle ganas.

– Oscar Cervantes

Oscar was born in a very small town in Jalisco, Mexico. The great majority of his family and relatives were either illiterate or had at the most an elementary school education. Oscar was blessed to be a first-generation college graduate. When he was seven years old, he began working full time in the farm and agricultural fields while attending elementary school. Oscar obtained a scholarship in order to attend the Catholic Seminary boarding junior and high school of the Dioceses of Zamora Michoacan.

While Oscar was still in elementary school, his father came to the United States in order to work in the fields of Northern California so he could support his family. Oscar, his mother, and six siblings eventually joined the father. Upon his high school graduation, Oscar and his family arrived in the San Francisco Bay area. Oscar did not speak English. He obtained a full scholarship at Saint Patrick's College Seminary. This college was the most supportive institution during his academic life. The college did not have an English as a second language program. However, Oscar was able to obtain a full scholarship and graduated in four years. Then, he obtained a Master of Sciences in clinical counseling from the California State University–Hayward. In addition, he obtained a PhD in clinical psychology from the California School of Professional Psychology–Berkeley. While obtaining his doctorate program, he encountered severe racism and discrimination. However, this made him stronger and led him into performing research, teaching, and consulting about issues of racism, and discrimination toward Latinos, and the development of programs in order to admit, retain, and graduate Latinos from college and graduate schools. Oscar founded and became faculty liaison for several Latino students' associations at several universities. Oscar became the director of multicultural affairs. He also took leadership roles such as president of the Latino faculty and staff at the University of Southern California as well as president of the California Hispanic Psychological Association. Oscar continued mentoring and supervising Latino medical students and medical residents while serving as a clinical professor at the UCSF School of Medicine. The great majority of his patients in private practice have been Latinos.

Unfortunately, there continues to be a digital divide in the Latino community. While the digital divide among cell phone and smartphone ownership continues to decrease, there still is a large gap among desktop or laptop computers ownership or internet use. Education decreases the gap. The higher the education and the higher the income, the more technology adoption and the more opportunities to be present at the decision-making table. Young Latinos experience less digital divide than older Latinos or those who primarily speak Spanish or did not obtain a high school diploma. Latino immigrants are overrepresented in frontline pandemic-response occupations, such as home health aides, grocery store clerks, and agricultural field workers, leaving them more exposed to COVID-19. Foreign-born Latinos have much lower levels of digital skills.

Telemedicine has been very practical in reaching the Latino community or those who live far away from major cities where it is very hard to find specialists. However, due to the digital divide, especially with migrant, Spanish mono-lingual, and elderly Latinos, the pandemic posed a great challenge. Thus, Oscar mentions relying on his cell phone to practice medicine and serve these communities.

Oscar lists three goals for his community: (1) increasing drastically the number of Latino medical students and Latino medical faculty in all medical schools, (2) increasing scholarships/fellowships for Latino medical students, and (3) promoting well-qualified Latino professionals in all medical hospitals and medical clinics, as well as in public and private health departments.

3

Game Plan
Latinx-Factor Leaders

Rosalía Zárate, PhD
Research Scientist in People Analytics
Facebook
The true measure of any society can be found in how
it treats its most vulnerable members.
— Mahatma Gandhi

SOME OF THE OBSTACLES ROSALÍA Zárate encountered in college
had to do with her experience as a Latina math major, being
a first-generation college/masters/doctoral graduate. Mathematics has always been an integral part of her life. Mathematics was a subject where her parents could provide assistance
despite their language barrier; it became their common language. Many students grow up fearing math, but Rosalía
grew up loving it; she found it challenging and exciting.
However, while applying to undergraduate programs, she

never considered majoring in math, although she excelled in the subject. She was unfamiliar with professions in mathematics; she neither had role models nor understand how it could be applied to the real world and, furthermore, her sisters (who also provided much guidance) did not know of others who fully understood the U.S. educational system (e.g., what different universities had to offer, how to get into graduate school, how to study, what research was, the importance of office hours and building a relationship with professors).

Arriving at the University of California, Santa Barbara, was overwhelming and a culture shock. As a Latina growing up in a more conservative household and community, going off to college far from home was beyond her parents' expectations. Rosalía grew up in Delano, in the California San Joaquin Valley, a place where many students have limited access to formal education. As long as she can remember, her parents would tell her and her sisters, "The key to success is education." Rosalía took her academics very seriously, knowing that whatever she learned could never be taken away from her and would only help her get to college and career pathways. Rosalía's parents, who immigrated from Mexico, have always worked in agriculture as farm workers and did not earn enough to live above the poverty line. The lack of accessibility and resources that her community of Delano had to offer became salient once Rosalía got to college.

On the first day of linear algebra, she noticed that she was the only Latinx student in a class of 30 students and one of only four females. Having been in predominantly female math courses in high school, she felt intimidated, discouraged, and underprepared. This affected her performance. Fortunately, a *Profesora* encouraged her to continue to pursue mathematics. She struggled her first year, and as time progressed, she grew accustomed to university coursework and her performance steadily improved. The resilience from her previous years began to resurface. This resilience helped her through undergraduate program, to gain admission to the Stanford Graduate School of Education and the Masters in Statistics program. Given her experience, Rosalía understands the struggle of being a first-generation college student, what it is like to be a woman in STEM (science, technology, engineering, and mathematics), balancing family, culture, and ambition. Rosalía continued to experience the emotions and challenges that numerous students share within our educational system as she transitioned into graduate school and then into the workforce in tech.

Rosalía's county (Kern) has been recognized as one of the most illiterate in this country, one of the most impoverished, and even the county with the worst air and water quality. However, it is also home of the United Farm Workers' movement, of some of the most hardworking, humble, and generous people she knows. Rosalía's community has so much *corazon* (heart) that they "make it happen" regardless of what cards are dealt to them.

Gracias a Dios (thank the Lord) and her parents' selflessness and determination, Rosalía was motivated to be a role model in her community and to continue to always move forward, *para adelante*. They motivated her to go on to graduate school and to pursue her dreams, whatever they may be, "*tu puedes*." And so she did.

When Rosalía thinks of the digital divide, she thinks of the lack of accessibility to technology, to understanding technology, to accessibility to computer science and engineering curricula. Rosalía thinks of rural and impoverished communities like her hometown of Delano, where one can only imagine what the digital divide looks like and how it has been exacerbated at this time, when students are struggling with logging in to class (where guardians at home may not know how to log them in to class or the guardian is an older sibling) and lack access to stable internet connections.

It is a divide that exists not only among our younger generations but also among older generations. Rosalía thinks about the divide that exists in understanding how a smartphone works, how email and computer software works. How our society has left older generations behind and out of the conversation about "technology" and the use of technology in our current society, and how our generation at times seems to be left out of the discussion regarding the creation and use of machine learning and artificial intelligence–related products. Rosalía thinks about her parents' generation and their anxiety in trying to understand how to maneuver a smartphone, not understanding how to set up an online account, and the challenge in trying to explain her data-related work to them (a heartfelt challenge).

How do we diminish this gap? In one of his interviews, Professor Yuval Harari is asked about what he foresees occurring in the space of education and what might need to change in the upcoming years if we want to move forward as the human race. He touches upon the importance of interdisciplinary work (e.g., checking in with one another as we bring in technology such as artificial intelligence into the healthcare system), and the need for empathy as we continue to live in this digital world, building and advancing in machine learning and artificial intelligence.

Rosalía agrees that Latinos/Latinx need to be interdisciplinary and work with one another as we try to address problems and provide solutions. There is no other way for us to move forward. Technology is present in all aspects of our lives, so if we want to move toward a more equitable and just society we must work together and we must do so with empathy. Rosalía advises that as we advance in technology, we have to make sure that technological creations do not negatively affect our Latinx community. All creations and advancements should be made with the most vulnerable in mind.

When Rosalía thinks of the digital divide in terms of lack of access to computer science courses, for example, she thinks of companies that are assisting by providing communities of color with more resources and exposure to coding. But there are not many who are investing in actually building culturally relevant computer science curriculum, helping teachers develop the curriculum, and training teachers to teach such courses. Rosalía worries about the divide between researchers, companies/investors, and practitioners.

How do we encourage Latinx students to pursue higher education? By reminding them that their stories, their perspectives, their talents and skills are valuable, powerful, and very much needed. In order to make sure that the needs of our Latinx community are being discussed we need to be present at the highest levels. As Rosalía's parents always remind her, education is power.

In order to ensure that we are represented, that we are considered, that our community issues and solutions are at the forefront, we need to be educated. We need to understand the issues our community faces, we need to continue to build our skillset to address these issues in all sectors, and we need to work together and share our knowledge to progress as a community because, sadly, if we are not present our community may continue to be overlooked (as can be seen throughout history and currently).

Having a PhD, for example, can open doors that one may have never even dreamed of or knew existed; it serves as a key to create change. Rosalía's doctoral program not only taught her about the educational challenges this country faces but also enabled her to work on some of the most critical issues our Latinx students face in their educational trajectories by providing them with the skills needed to find solutions. As a doctoral candidate, Rosalía mentions one is responsible for and looked to, to create something new – a new method, a new theory, a new perspective or way of analyzing a problem. As a PhD you would have the skillset to be able to do that, to see your vision through from inception to completion and to serve as a voice for those who are most vulnerable or do not have access to the privileges of a doctoral workspace. Also, think about the impact of seeing someone from your background with a doctoral degree or as a professor. How many Latinx professors did you have in college; probably not many? Think about the impact that had on you, and how you can now get to be that person for another student.

Rosalía promotes diversity, equity, and inclusion by making sure that it's on every agenda that she has access to.

Whatever groups you're part of, whatever project you're working on, make sure that diversity, equity, and inclusion are at the forefront.

Rosalía promotes diversity, equity, and inclusion by taking action. Whenever she is on any job, she will make sure to ask questions related to diversity, equity, and inclusion – what are the goals, milestones related to achieving a diverse workforce, what does diversity look like, what does inclusion look like, and how will success in these areas be measured? Rosalía promotes it by making it a part of her everyday life – general conversations, sharing knowledge from the books she read in relation to diversity in tech and the effect of biased algorithms on communities of color, including the Latinx community: Rosalía makes it a part of her daily work and research. Rosalía also makes sure to speak to younger generations about college, graduate school, and the need for their skills and talents in STEM fields.

Rosalía promotes diversity, equity and inclusion by having conversations highlighting how now, more than ever, our perspectives are needed.

If we want to make any advances in tech and we want to make sure that our technology is unbiased, then we need to make sure that our workplaces accurately represent the communities they are trying to serve. Individuals developing technology need to be aware of their unconscious biases and how those biases may be reflected in the products they create – hence the need for a diverse talent.

Also, it's important to consider that machine learning works by utilizing historical data. If the historical data is biased, then the outcome will be biased; the results or output are simply a reflection of what has been input. Thus, if we want that to change we need to make sure that the data we collect is representative of the community we are trying to serve. The data should make sense; this can be checked by making sure that our research or product designs are correctly piloted with diverse populations, that survey items are tested, that we work with the communities we are creating products for. Researchers and companies, for example, should work with practitioners and their local communities to confirm that their interpretations of particular instruments make sense. Those collecting data need to check in with one another throughout their data-collecting process and take note of how different people may be responding to a product or survey of interest – do all participants understand the survey questions, are we capturing the information we actually want, who is/is not being surveyed, who is responding as expected/or differently than expected, and why might that be? Thus, we also need to ensure that we have a diverse set of eyes analyzing and utilizing the data.

In order for individuals including Latinx students to succeed in higher education they need to build a community of support because one cannot achieve success by oneself. This includes building study groups, connecting with a community that they can relate to where they feel that they belong (for Rosalía, that was Los Ingenieros/MESA organization in undergrad), finding mentors and role models across different areas. Rosalía was a math major who was interested in education, so she sought out mentors in those fields. It was challenging at times to approach professors/professionals, so it is helpful to remember that the majority of the time, people want to help and that it does not hurt to ask.

One of the greatest challenges for Rosalía in graduate school was feeling like she didn't belong and that she did not have much to contribute, at least not compared to her peers. "How could she possibly be Stanford material?" Rosalía would ask herself. She was the youngest in one of her cohorts of about 30 doctoral students, and one of maybe two, if not the only, first-generation Latina in her PhD program and masters (in statistics) program. Building a community of support, finding mentors, and realizing that you do have much to offer helped her to feel as though she did belong at Stanford, in the research space, in academia, and in all spaces. Her voice matters.

It is important for students to take care of their health – mentally, physically, and emotionally. Undergraduate and graduate studies, and now the professional workplace, come with their challenges. Some may include dealing with imposter syndrome, cultural dissonance, fear of failure, comparing yourself to others, being too hard on yourself, being impatient with your growth, and managing multicultural worlds. Having a community of support definitely helps with this, as does reaching out to a therapist or counselor to help you process these experiences that many encounter. Also, it is okay to take a break from school if needed, but work on having a plan and having a person(s) to hold you accountable to your plan/goals.

In regards to funding, in addition to seeking scholarships and grants, if one needs to work they should look into work study, and for research assistantships and teaching assistantships that may be available at the undergraduate and graduate levels. This also highlights the importance of building relationships with professors/professionals and other students – build your network. At times professors/professionals may offer contract work; reach out to those you may be interested in working with! Ideally, students should seek opportunities where they can develop/apply skills in their field of interest. Students within our community might not know what they're interested in or might not have been exposed to different fields; therefore, networking, reaching out to individuals for informal chats on LinkedIn, for example, can help in learning about different fields and opportunities/career paths.

It is important for Latinx students to step outside of their comfort zone, which might need to happen often, because in many instances they may be in uncharted territories because not many Latinxs may have walked a similar path. Additionally, because we are still underrepresented at the undergraduate and graduate level, it is critical that we all work together, look after one another, focus on positive impact, and find the allies.

At times we are scared of failure, one should remember that this is part of our growth and that we are not expected to solve all of the problems in our community, nor do we represent all of the voices in our community – take that weight off of your shoulders. Don't shut your own doors – sometimes we are our own worst enemy – instead, apply to the job, to the internship, to the college of choice.

And, most important, in order for Latinxs to succeed we need to remain humble, grounded, continue to help others, remember where we come from, be kind, and do our work with integrity. This all can help us make real progress by staying true to ourselves and our personal and communal goals.

Bryan Osorio
Mayor
City of Delano

Not everything that is faced can be changed, but nothing can be changed until it is faced.

— James Baldwin

Bryan Osorio grew up in Delano, California. He was born in Orange County, but his family moved a few hours north to the City of Delano when he was around seven years old. Bryan went through the public schools in Delano, and he really owes his opportunities of applying to college to his parents, then-girlfriend, and high school counselor. Because his parents immigrated to the United States at a young age, they did not finish high school, but they always wanted him to excel in school so that, when the time came, he could be eligible for college.

Bryan's mom, especially, was very supportive and pushed him to do the best that he could. His girlfriend, during his senior year of high school, was a bright, successful, and ambitious student. She actually motivated him to apply to UC Berkeley, which he had never heard of. And his high school counselor connected him to SAT waivers, designated a time for his class to start applying for colleges, and helped him with FAFSA questions. With their help, he ended up successfully applying to college on an iPad that his parents had won in a raffle.

So, in the fall of 2014, he began his studies at University of California, Berkeley. It was very tough being away from his home and dealing with imposter syndrome. It is not the norm for Delano high school students to go away for college or even finish college. Bryan believes the latest statistic for Delano is that only 7 percent of students have a bachelor's degree or higher. On top of the academic rigor, it was difficult focusing in school at times with the presidential election and administration of Donald Trump, who vilified people like his family. In time, he found a community of friends and colleagues who were interested in public service that helped to mold him into an advocate. By the end of the spring of 2018, he was the first college graduate in his family.

The digital divide is an incredibly significant issue in the Latino/a/x community and is one that continues to be highlighted during the COVID-19 pandemic. In Bryan's city, where poverty and unemployment rates are relatively high, broadband access is a luxury that several families sometimes choose to not have for the sake of saving money. Moreover, the knowledge of how to use technology is not to be taken for granted. Retroactively, Bryan believes we should have changed the narrative by bringing in different stakeholders who have seen and heard of the digital divide in Delano, in order to strategize how we will lessen the divide. Now, he believes it is time we highlight the stories of kids whose pandemic-year school hotspot is the first time they had broadband access at home. Bryan thinks it is time we raise the concerns of pricing. And, Bryan thinks it is time we prioritize tackling the digital divide within our city.

Bryan ran for office because he wanted to see representation that championed social justice and advocated for our marginalized communities. Bryan was not seeing that locally, especially in such a politicized time. So, a few months after graduating from college in 2018, Bryan announced his candidacy for the Delano City Council. With the help of volunteers and friends, especially his campaign manager, Angelica Rodriguez, who was a senior at UC Berkeley, he was able to win the most votes in his election at the age of 22.

Bryan is currently the mayor for the City of Delano, California. In his first year on the council, he asked his local government to make city council meetings more accessible online, especially as larger cities have been streaming their meetings online. Since the pandemic started in 2020, their city of 53,000, as well as many others, has meetings that are accessible through Zoom and viewable through Facebook. Moreover, he wishes to make sure they can grant more technological and broadband access to their youth by further utilizing their Technology Center, and he has made it a goal to accomplish this by the end of his term. Ultimately, they have a lot of work to do as local leaders in ensuring their community can be educated and provided technology access.

Bryan strongly believes that as a Latino/Latinx community, they can succeed when they see and realize that there is more that unites "us" than divides us. As cliche as that statement may sound, he truly believes in it, because there are so many issues impacting marginalized communities, including the Latino, Black, LGBTQ+, immigrant, and other communities. Yet, sometimes, in our own community, we clash with each other on different issues. Bryan understands we are not a monolith. But, at the end of the day, we have to remember our history and how our ancestors fought hard against systems of oppression in order to pave the way for us to continue paving the way for more inclusivity and change for future generations.

Our Latino community continues struggling through structural inequalities that not only impact Latinos but also other vulnerable groups. Bryan believes that through understanding our intersectional struggles and uniting as a collective group we can mobilize and we can achieve success.

Leeanna Chipana
Adjunct Professor
Fashion Institute of Technology

Art will save you.

— Leeanna Chipana

Leeanna Chipana grew up in Central Islip, Long Island, New York. She is a first-generation college graduate. Her father was born in Peru in the mountains. He was an indigenous man and spoke Quechua. He went to school only up to the sixth grade. After that he had to work to support the family. When he was older, he made his way to Lima and learned to speak Spanish, saved money, and immigrated to New York. This meant that while growing up, Leeanna's father actually looked to her to know the correct thing to do here in America. As a child she had to be an adult right away to help her parents. She struggled in school because, essentially, she had to figure everything out on her own. There was no parent to say, "Hey, looks like you need tutoring in math."

There was no parent to help with her homework, and schools do not teach kids basic life management skills. She was totally on her own. She could see her father had a lot of pride. "He would never ask for help or show people he really didn't know how to do something, so there was a pride with me as well." Leeanna did not ask for help or did not know how to ask for help in school. She didn't understand she even *could* ask for help. Leeanna did not plan on applying to colleges as a teen because she assumed it was for other kids who had parents with money to help them. The concept of a loan or a grant was not in her sphere of knowledge at all. Leeanna had a guidance counselor who pushed her to apply. When she got to college, she did not know basic things like time management, how to prioritize what to work on or how to study, how to pay bills, and so forth, so she struggled a lot in college. She recalls thinking, "Okay, suddenly you are supposed to be a complete adult and automatically somehow know all of these things." Leeanna also had undiagnosed ADHD, so her studies were very difficult.

As a teacher, she can see the stark difference between those students who have always had access to a knowledgeable, educated adult and those who are trying to figure it all out on their own. She sees these traits mirrored in her own experiences; having been completely overwhelmed in college, she failed courses her first year. It was not until her final year that she felt she had a good grasp of her studies and was able to make straight A's.

In her academic experience, teaching at various colleges in New York, she still does not see enough diversity. You need diversity to change the culture within an organization to be more equitable. Some are trying, but more is still needed to reach parity.

Leeanna feels that when a person is starting out as an adjunct it would be nice if there were a community specifically designed to help him or her navigate the academic community. She imagines that in this community, you are assigned a mentor and you meet with them monthly online and can reach out to them any time. Then Leeanna can see them getting into decision-making roles more quickly.

Leeanna only recently became involved in "Hispanic" online communities. Growing up, her father refused to teach her Quechua or Spanish because he wanted her to be as "American" as possible. She believes you may find many Latinx individuals who are disconnected from any sort of Hispanic Community. She personally has never felt comfortable calling herself Hispanic, Latina, or Spanish. Leeanna identifies as Quechuan-American, which makes her Native-American, not Native American (there's a difference). She would like to see a change in the wording of these groups to be something more like LNSCA (Latinx, Native South and Central Americans). Much like the LGBTQ community, the Latinx community is extremely diverse in how people identify. The words "Latina" and "Hispanic," in Leeanna's view, have too many ties to colonialism. Leeanna thinks this acronym would include more people, and establish a foundation on which to build more mentorship programs that will lead to academic and career success.

Leeanna has gotten into art also to show inclusivity. However, Leeanna believes the problem is when immigrant parents hear the word "art," they think their children are fingerpainting in an art class. The word has a bad reputation. They may not understand that it is used everywhere, is part of every product they buy, and furthermore is integral to their students' brain development. Numerous studies show how the arts help students learn to become better problem solvers. Leeanna would suggest incorporating art that uses technology, like classes in product design or 3D sculpture, and digital drawing and painting. So, every art class incorporates tech. This way, students are still creating and "'making," which teaches them problem-solving skills and at the same time learning the tech used in the real world right now.

With art one can create a visual representation of what they are thinking about, what they are struggling with, or what they are currently investigating. Through social media platforms we communicate to one other with our art. We tell each other pages of information without saying any words. The social media posts say, *Hey, this is what Leeanna is thinking about.* Right now, she sees a lot of Latinx artists investigating their identity and reclaiming their ancestry. Leeanna sees strong indigenous women in Brazil and Peru fighting for their land against developers and winning. There is a sense of empowerment that comes with art when we see ourselves represented. When she sees activist Nemonte Nenquimo as a heroine on the cover of *Time* magazine, or actress Yalitza Aparicio winning awards, Leeanna is more empowered herself. To Leeanna this is crucial for the future of Latinx people. She has spent a long time trying to be what she thought a "Latina" was supposed to be, and so she played into stereotypes seen in media. Now, she looks up to real women, like Nemonte and Yalitza, and through her own art she unearths more and more of who she is, and feels that her identity is in "my hands now, no one else's."

There is a lot of colorism and racism in the Latin community. Leeanna states that it's really obvious when you go to

Peru and see all the men in their business suits at lunch. You can clearly see the divide between the men with Spanish ancestry in power positions and the indigenous men in the laborer roles. Her own father's self-esteem was greatly affected by this. He always felt very small when he was around other Peruvian men of Spanish descent. That kind of thinking is very pervasive in the home and will affect the children of these immigrant families. It took many, many years for Leeanna to simply be okay with how she looked and to shake away the shame she always felt. Leeanna paints against the battle of racism, and the self-hate born from it. Leeanna hopes to empower women of Central and South American indigenous ancestry. Through her art she wants them to hear, *Hey, I see you, you are important, and you are not alone.*

Leeanna believes Latinx professors can go to their diversity administrators and open up a discussion about Latinx students. In her required diversity training workshops, she has yet to see thorough discussion on the specific needs of children of immigrant parents.

Leeanna imagines official pdf packets from high school principals that explain in Spanish small but very important things parents can do, like requiring their child bring them their grades on paper and not only tell them their grades. They may not know this is an option. Or perhaps a group that does home visits to discuss with parents important study habits they can help their kids with. Parents may be working too much to actually be that involved, but if they learn some strategies on how to teach their children accountability or roles they can take on in the home, this would make an impact.

Elizabeth Kukka
Executive Director
Ethereum Classic Labs

A candle never loses any of its light while lighting up another candle.

— Rumi

Elizabeth Kukka was born and raised in San José, California – her parents still live in the same house today, in a working-class community on the west side. She and her sisters were not only the first in the family to graduate from college, but also the first in the neighborhood. There was an expectation that they would go to university – *no matter what.* Yet, they also had no idea how they would get there. The application process, SATs, and internships were a mystery. In 1998, in preparation for the "big test," she remembers asking her mom to take her to Barnes & Noble to buy an SAT prep book. Today, a teen is likely to be enrolled in prep courses and have tutors lined-up or study groups to meet with. In addition to practicing on her own, she attended a free college-prep workshop. It was there that she learned about scholarships, how to fill out a college application, and took a mock SAT exam – it had a dozen or so questions on it, far fewer than the number of prep questions most teens use for practice.

When deciding which schools to apply to, the ones closest to home were prioritized – keeping the family close together was important to her parents. At the time, she evaluated a school by its numeric ranking, and where she thought she fit-in based on her average GPA. Never did I think to inquire about opportunities like internships, letters of recommendation, introductions, or networking.

College was fun – Elizabeth made new friends and loved learning at San Francisco State University. Yet, she was also floundering a bit. Changing majors four times, visiting school counselors, and taking advantage of office hours – the idea of commitment was terrifying. For example, did she want to do the same job for the rest of her life, and what if she didn't like it? She was unsure of which questions to ask, or how to ask for direction and guidance. What was she going to do after graduation? She needed a mentor, or two, without knowing it, and didn't know where to find one.

Fast-forward eight years: Elizabeth had graduated from SFSU, became a successful public-school teacher, and then decided to go back to school for her MBA – against her parents' wishes and to their horror and trepidation. Why couldn't she just be grateful for her stable job? Why shoot for the unknown and take on a large financial risk? For a solid two years, she was met with uncertainty and doubt, and her parents suffered regret, felt on her behalf. Finishing her MBA in 2016, she successfully transitioned from education to tech, while having just as much fun, by facing a new type of challenge. And her parents are finally proud of her, once again.

Sometimes you need to believe in yourself when no one else will, individuals, companies, institutions, and policymakers, and just be your own champion. She believes there are five keys for Latinos to focus on to continue to progress in Latino evolution.

1. Early exposure to digital career paths
2. Teamwork

3. Relationship building
4. Go the extra mile
5. Company hierarchy and negotiation

EARLY EXPOSURE TO DIGITAL CAREER PATHS

You don't know what you don't know. Within an academic setting, a few ways to expose Latino and Latinx students to a broader array of career paths include field trips to tech companies, bringing in guest speakers, and attending online events.

TEAMWORK

One place to learn to work as a team is to play team sports! Team sports teach about cooperation and direct, accurate communication. Sports also teach us how to celebrate small victories: a great pass, cross, or catch. It teaches friendly competition, to win while also being able to admire and acknowledge the skills and successes of others. Exercise also boosts endorphins, which make us feel happy. When work is stressful, bringing a positive attitude can go a long way.

RELATIONSHIP BUILDING

Learn active communication and listening skills. If you come from a large family, like Elizabeth's, then everyone may be yelling over each other, trying to be heard. Taking time for your colleagues, learning about their interests and what they are working on, goes a long way.

GO THE EXTRA MILE

Take your deliverables one or two steps further; put together process documents that are badly needed but no one is tasked to complete; stay on top of industry trends by reading, listening to podcasts, and attending industry talks and conferences. In the workplace, ask your organization to purchase corporate subscriptions to magazines like *MIT Technology Review* or *Harvard Business Review*.

COMPANY HIERARCHY AND NEGOTIATION

Learning to ask the right questions during an interview will save you time and a headache. Understanding a company's structure will reveal growth opportunities. And, speaking with current and former employees can be helpful. Practicing difficult conversations can also be useful. For example, stating during an interview "I would like to lead a team within the next six months to a year. Is there a path to help make this happen?" Or, negotiating a six-month performance review for an increase in title and responsibility. For the latter, you may need to bring the conversation up on your own, advocate for yourself, and not expect anyone to do you any favors. It's great if it happens, but don't wait for someone to give you what you want.

Elizabeth's organization runs multiple businesses, so she has had a few titles, including executive director at Ethereum Classic Labs, principal investor at Digital Finance Group, and director at Digital Custody, Inc. Equity and inclusion are embedded into our business by ensuring that we have a diverse pool of candidates when interviewing, having balanced representation on our teams, and ensuring that we work with partners, investors, start-ups, and vendors who have a similar philosophy.

"Blockchain is a fairly diverse vertical, and it's the most globally minded industry that I've ever been a part of." There's representation from every corner of the world which contributes to the variety of languages, cultures, and ethnicities participating in chat groups, social channels, and speaking at conferences. Although it is male heavy, like the majority of tech, there are many female leaders like Catherine Coley, US-CEO at Binance; Amiti Uttarwar, bitcoin core developer; Elizabeth Stark, CEO at Lightning Labs; and Aya Miyaguchi, executive director at Ethereum Foundation.

Latinos can dive into blockchain by becoming familiar with the industry. Start out by reading articles by The Block, CoinDesk, CoinTelegraph, and Messari Crypto. Check out podcasts like The Pomp, What Bitcoin Did, and UnChained. Attend one of the many virtual meet-ups and go to an annual Ethereum conference like ETH San Francisco, Denver, New York, Paris, or Berlin, when the world opens up again after the pandemic. Blockchain really has something for everyone, from buying crypto, to mining, to deep-tech research like algorithm design, distributed systems, or decentralized storage. There are solutions for enterprise, solutions developed by enterprise, and solutions that expand across verticals into agtech, healthtech, insurtech, and of course, fintech. Only recently did she find out that it's a "nerdy" industry – all this time she thought they were the cool kids!

Sondra Jenzer
Nonprofit Development and Fundraising Consultant

Do the best you can until you know better. Then, when you know better, do better.

– Maya Angelou

At six years old Sondra Jenzer was adopted from an orphanage in El Salvador by a single American woman. Upon arriving to adopt her, her mother discovered she had a half sister who was also in the orphanage and adopted them both. For 12 years following her adoption, her mother reassured the sisters that they would return to visit their birth family in El Salvador.

Sondra's formative years in an orphanage and seeing the devastation every time she went back to visit the war-ravaged country subconsciously solidified her social-impact path. If she were to base her going to college on her birth family's history, she would be a first-generation college student, but the reality is that without being adopted it would simply not have been an opportunity in her life. Being adopted afforded her all the privileges that she never even knew she could dream about. Sondra was fortunate to have a teacher for a mother, so there was never any doubt she would go to college.

She entered college as a second-generation college student, but it was not easy for her. Her senior year of high school, her mother was diagnosed with breast cancer and had a co-occurring health condition that made her cancer terminal. During Sondra's second semester of college her mother died; she was 18 years old. Her mother's death after only a short 12 years together was a traumatic experience that took almost a decade to overcome. In the immediate aftermath of her death, she failed three classes and subsequently had to attend summer classes to make up the credits to be able to stay on track to graduate on time.

There is no doubt in Sondra's mind that her former years in the orphanage, being ostracized because of her Latina background in a predominantly Irish-Italian neighborhood in the suburbs of Brooklyn, and being adopted and speaking only Spanish as she entered her first educational experience in an all-English-speaking school at six and a half years old, were the elixir that gave her the strength, perseverance, and drive to harness the pain to work for her. When you go through the fire at a young age, whether you realize it or not, you are equipped with an emotional and mental armor that you would not have had without those tough life experiences. Going through that fire shaped who she is today, and guided her toward the nonprofit work that she is in.

For years, the digital divide has placed many marginalized and underserved communities at a disadvantage, and the pandemic has accelerated and widened this gap. The Latino/x community is no exception. There is no doubt by now that the future is digital. What this means for the many Latino and Latinx households that come from lower socioeconomic and/or immigrant backgrounds is that they are losing valuable time operating without the same resources and opportunities as their more affluent (often white) counterparts. This means they have already begun their life with one hand tied behind their back and yet are expected to deliver on and achieve the same expectations. This is not equitable.

Sondra's work in the nonprofit sector (or for-impact organizations, as I like to refer to them) seeks to drive transformative change by working with organizations whose mission is to provide programs and services that advance equity so everyone may be given the same access to education, health, employment, housing, nutrition, a support system, and technology, irrespective of their background.

The importance of digital inclusion cannot be underestimated, and nonprofits are in a unique position to implement

solutions to many of these local, regional, and national discon-
nects. With technology progressing and changing at record
speeds, barriers to telework, telehealth, connecting with a support system, and virtual/distance learning puts the Latino/x
community at an extreme disadvantage. Whether through a
lack of access to the internet, laptops, or a network that can help
them tap into and guide them on how to leverage online networks, the chasm for the Latino/x community must be addressed.

But while nonprofits are in the best position to provide the
necessary community support on the ground, with insight
into the myriad of challenges these communities experience,
in nonprofit work the Latino/x community is barely a conversation. This needs to change. We must be at the table, and
that means supporting current nonprofit Latino/x leaders
not only in the work they are doing through programs and
services but also in their ability to cultivate Latino/x leaders
both in their organizations and in the broader community.
People and technology are the main drivers that are expo-
nentially propelling businesses and organizations forward,
working hand in hand to accelerate each other. Therefore,
funders and other supporters should invest in and consider
leadership cultivation and innovative technological tools as
a valuable return on their social impact investment. Most
important, we must see Latino/x individuals reflected in
CEOs, staffs, boards, and as community leaders, and we must
create an entire network around these groups on a local,
regional, and national level.

One of the best examples Sondra has ever experienced
around diversity, equity, and inclusion was during her time in
Western Samoa as a Community Development volunteer
with the Peace Corps. To be able to progress into the

two-year program, volunteers were required to participate in a three-month language and cultural training that set the framework and foundation of how they were going to do their work. This was critical in approaching their work with a level of sensitivity and awareness that opened their eyes and hearts to the needs of the community they intended to serve. Since then, everything she has done has been through a diversity, equity, and inclusion lens. And it is this lens that ensures her nonprofit and community development is always people-centric. Having worked in the nonprofit and social entrepreneurship space for more than 10 years, she is passionate and skilled in developing and implementing community development programs, and measuring their impact, in conjunction with finding the revenue sources to support them.

Recently, Sondra embarked on her entrepreneurial journey, providing services to emerging and small nonprofits around analysis, and advising foundations and frameworks to create, develop, scale, and sustain missions. While the core of her work is with nonprofits, in strategic relationships and revenue solutions, her perspective and approach are holistic and integrative, underpinned by an iterative process that zeros in on a cross-functional, collaborative team model; program impact, monitoring, and evaluation methods and processes; creating, developing, and sustaining revenue models that leverage organizational assets; a team-centric foundation and process; and technology as a foundational tool to scale and grow.

The reality is that nonprofits are underresourced, understaffed, and underfunded, and traditionally are behind the digital and technology curve in comparison to other sectors. This means that many teams are overstretched and – if not already there – are headed toward burnout. Combined with the reality that many nonprofit teams are also not receiving the professional development they need that can empower them to do the best job possible, nonprofits generally are at an enormous disadvantage. Leveraging technology can alleviate some of these organizational challenges by increasing impact and scaling organizations in ways never possible before. This is why a key component of her work is mentoring nonprofits in their use of technology, emphasizing innovations and new systems in the technology field that can support their endeavors, and, more important, accelerate their work.

From their tools in programming, monitoring, and evaluation to accepting bitcoins from donors, the faster nonprofits can embrace and leverage technology, the bigger the impact they can have. In fact, Sondra predicts that nonprofits that are challenged to embrace and leverage technology quickly enough – either by design or default – will be at an enormous disadvantage compared to emerging nonprofits that are led by digital natives and integrate technology into their strategic communication and growth plan from the onset.

Representation matters, networks are key, and mentors are integral in supporting the next generation of leaders and the current change-makers. The reality is that this simply does not exist en masse in the Latino/Latinx community as it does elsewhere, and we cannot put the onus on younger generations when we know from experience how challenging this can be. We need to continue to build online and offline communities, and we need to find ways to build bridges across those networks. Es Tiempo is an organization doing just that!

4

Inclusion

Executive Nonprofit Leadership and Education

Anna María Chávez
Chief Impact Officer and President
Encantos.org
If you're not doing one thing that you're scared about every day, you're not growing.

— Anna María Chávez

ANNA MARÍA CHÁVEZ GREW UP in rural southern Arizona with her father, a migrant farmworker, and her mother, who ran a large farm nearby. They were both leaders in her community — volunteering, offering guidance, and showing her what public service looked like day in and day out. They valued education and knew that a good one would open opportunities for her. Anna María's grandmother, who had not received a formal education, reinforced this message and taught her never to take this privilege for granted. So even though she attended an underfunded school, typical of a small farm town in Arizona, and was a first-generation college student, she had a support system that encouraged her to get everything and more out of it and a home life that taught her the things her classes could not: what it meant to help your neighbors, lead by example, and fight for your community.

The term *digital divide* was coined 25 years ago, so it is not a new problem. Rather, it has been an issue in the Latino community for a long time. The COVID-19 pandemic and the shift to online learning highlighted the disparities in technology and internet access for our Latino, Black, and indigenous students and intensify the impact. The digital divide plagues students and families in urban, suburban, and rural communities. Nationwide, an estimated 16 million students lack reliable access to high-speed broadband.

Throughout the pandemic, we have seen how communities are innovating to serve their students – from districts using their school buses as mobile internet hotspots, to public school teachers speaking from radio stations or local television stations to bring learning into the homes of their students. School boards, superintendents, and educators are doing everything possible to help overcome the digital divide's disproportionate impact on our nation's Black, Brown, and low-income students.

Our public schools need help – from short-term solutions like donations and support for tech equipment and extended Wi-Fi access, to long-term funding solutions.

The nationwide shift to remote and hybrid forms of delivering instruction has spurred some innovative developments and led public education down a path where instruction can be more personalized to students' unique needs and meet them where they are. This is the focus of Ad Astra Media – creating educational STEM content to help teach and inspire youth and adults from Latino and underserved communities. But so many students are still not able to access that innovation. Why? Because to "be at the decision-making table" we must talk about it but, equally important, we must take action. One way to do that is to encourage Latino parents and caregivers to run for their local school board. Today, 78 percent of all school board members in the United States are white.

We also need to encourage our communities to talk with their state and local representatives to share what is important for our Latino families and children. By keeping the spotlight on the unique needs of our school children, we can drive change.

In June 2020, Anna María became the Executive Director and Chief Executive Officer of the National School Boards Association (NSBA), a federation of state associations and the U.S. Virgin Islands that represents over 90,000 locally elected and appointed school board officials serving over 50 million public school children. Working with and for our members, NSBA advocates for equity and excellence in public education through school board leadership. To advance that mission, serve our members, and champion educational equity, Anna María leads a team of policy, member services, legal, communications, and business experts.

The NSBA believe all students should have access to an education that maximizes their individual potential. As advocates of educational equity, they equip our members with resources, research, and other supports they can use to advance their work with the local school boards.

To help guide and propel their equity work, NSBA launched the Transformation Now! initiative that puts our public school students and their individual needs at the center of learning and sets out to reinvent public schooling in the United States, close the digital divide, and prepare students with the twenty-first-century knowledge and skills they need to succeed. Ad Astra Media creates bilingual STEM informed resources to further this mission.

A major pillar of this transformation is addressing the systemic, institutional racism housed within schools and inscribed within our education policy. In 2020, NSBA established the Dismantling Institutional Racism in Education (DIRE) initiative, which provides a framework for confronting the myriad ways racism presents itself in education – from explicit bias and the overdisciplining of Black and Brown students to the chronic underfunding of schools in low-income communities of color. The exact dynamics of educational inequity are unique to every school. DIRE equips local school boards and decision-makers in education to build smart policy on a foundation of data and research. It helps support work to confront the realities of local education systems and construct and implement responsive solutions that work. Data, research, and a commitment to the creation and enactment of intentional policies that eliminate racism will help set the stage for a more equitable education system.

When Anna María was a young girl, she watched her mother run for a seat on the local school board at a time when it was unusual for women, especially Latina women, to seek elected office, let alone win a seat. Anna María had the chance to learn from her mother's example as she changed the world around her. Anna María was incredibly fortunate. Mentorship is critical for young people aspiring to be bigger than they can dream, and she had her mother, father, grandmother, teachers, and many other people who kicked down barriers for her. They showed Anna María what it meant to work for what she believes in and to weave public service into every day and every interaction. Anna María hopes that she is paving the way for more Latina women and women of color to lead organizations with missions that they are passionate about. There are always going to be obstacles, no matter who you are or where you come from. But when it comes down to it, what matters most is having people around you who believe in you and support your dreams and aspirations.

Amanda Renteria
CEO
Code for America

Mis suenos son tus suenos– "My dreams are your dreams." It's a way of remembering that the path Amanda walks is because generations before set those dreams in place. . . and I too, am setting the foundation for the next generation to keep dreaming.

– Amanda Renteria

Amanda Renteria grew up in the Central Valley of California. Her parents were former farmworkers. Amanda's dad came from Zacatecas, Mexico, and her mom from Santa

Ana, California. They landed in Woodlake because there was a popular farm labor camp just outside of town called Redbanks. That town, Woodlake, is in one of the poorest congressional districts in the state, among the 10th poorest across the country, literacy rates hover around 40 percent, unemployment is often in the double digits, and, as you might guess, the public schools are severely underresourced.

Therefore, it was a bit of a surprise her senior year when she received an acceptance package from Stanford University. There had been only three other students who had been accepted to Stanford in the history of her high school. And there had never been a woman, a Latino/Hispanic, or a daughter of farmworkers.

While she was excited about the opportunity, she really didn't know if she could do it – academically, financially, or logistically. Her family didn't buy into the "going away to college" theory. In fact, her dad was a pretty conservative Mexican father with three daughters, the kind of dad who lectured their prom dates for two hours before allowing them to go. You can imagine that, for Amanda's parents, Stanford felt like a planet away.

So, she leaned on her academic community to guide her through her decision-making process – teachers, coaches, and counselors. As she asked and listened, she could hear their concern. Everyone was certainly well meaning, but she could hear the subtle message that maybe Stanford was a bit too challenging for her, that "someone like her" might not be able to handle the academic rigor at Stanford. Although she was a confident kid, the consistent message was beginning to sink in, that maybe Stanford was a step too far. Then, her economics teacher pulled her aside before class and said,

"Listen, I know you're hearing all kinds of things about what you should or shouldn't do. But I'm here to tell you that it's not about you, it's about your community, and that someone like them can succeed at a place like that. You have to go."

When you hear the right words, even at 17, they ring in a different way. She said she knew she had to go. And, so, she took the leap. There's no doubt Stanford was hard. In fact, she learned pretty quickly the challenges she faced as she walked into her first calculus class. She sat at her desk and looked up at a busy calculus-infused chalkboard. She knew Spanish and English, but she didn't know *that* language.

So, after class, she walked up to the professor and asked, "Can you tell me where I can find your introductory class?" The professor looked a bit confused and said, "This is our entry level class." Then, he gracefully guided her over to the teacher's assistant, who handed her a thick book that she would need to study before, after, and in between the classes, just to catch up.

Amanda remembers the walk that day from the lecture hall to her dorm room, that sinking feeling of not knowing exactly how she was going to make it through. She couldn't call her parents and talk with them. She was too embarrassed to tell her roommate that the book in her backpack wasn't for the class, but just to prepare to be in the class. But, as she kept walking, she thought about the words of her economics teacher. He was right: she wasn't just holding that backpack, it was an entire community holding that backpack. And, she admits, over the course of the first year, she held *a lot* of extra books. But in the end, she figured it out.

Amanda double-majored in economics and political science. She also performed for the Ballet Folklorico de Stanford dancing group. She walked on to, not one, but two division one athletic teams and earned an athletic scholarship. And she did finally graduate . . . with honors. But how do we continue the evolution of Latino digital intelligence?

First, let's begin with access. Amanda explains we need to make sure that every family has the ability to get online and has devices and systems that allow for quality access and connection. It took until 2017 for her old high school to finally achieve full digital access for every student. This story is not an unusual one for rural, poor, marginalized Latinx communities.

Second, the only way to understand the deep level of inequality faced by the Latinx community is to incorporate Latinx talent at the decision-making table and trust their lived experience to shape policy and action. This requires a real commitment to listening and learning from and with community members themselves. She has learned over the course of her career, most poignant as the first Latina Chief of Staff in the U.S. Senate, that there are far too few of us at leadership tables in every industry. As a result, there has been an overall lack of attention or understanding about the issues that impact Latinx communities across the country. Therefore, Amanda emphasizes that we need a ramp-up in people and experiences that can foster a deeper understanding in and with Latinx communities.

Third, in 2020, the Latinx population became the largest ethnic minority group in the country. Consequently, the economic, social, and political rise or fall of the Latinx community will have reverberating impacts on the overall state of our country. Therefore, as we enter a world more reliant on digital access, it has never been more important to close the digital divide in Latinx/Hispanic communities.

Amanda is the CEO of Code for America, a nonprofit organization that partners with government to build equitable services for all, with a special focus on low-income programs. To be more specific, they are a tech support and providing powerful resources #GetCalFresh, #GetYourRefund, and #ClearMyRecord, as well as the network of Code for America civic tech volunteers in 90 chapters across the country. Their work is committed to helping government improve outreach and access to marginalized, low-income communities. They center for the people the government intends to serve, which means that they sit in social service centers with clients, visit families at home as they fill out forms, and listen to the obstacles people face when trying to access critical government services. From those experiences, they build what is needed to reach people with dignity and respect, putting people at the very center of research, product design, policy implementation, and anything they build for governments. Their belief is that it is not just about moving from paper to online, it's about utilizing tech to see and serve all people, especially those who have been left out for far too long.

Amanda's blog is called "Our Opportunity to Build a More Equitable Government" (https://www.codeforamerica.org/news/our-opportunity-to-build-a-more-equitable-government).

It's important to learn the system, and then to learn how to push the system toward justice for all. For too long, people have peddled the notion that government can't work, isn't innovative, or is just a clock-in, clock-out job.

Based on Amanda's experience, it is what we make of it. And, today, there's a once-in-a-generation opportunity to reimagine how government works and for whom. We need more people to drive a new vision for and in government and see ourselves as responsible for making that change. The last year of uncertainty due to a pandemic, economic challenges, and racial injustices should be a calling to every single person in this country to help create a country and government we can all be proud of, Amanda adds. She is hopeful that more people have come to understand the fragility of our democracy, the need for good government, the requirement to have efficient and effective systems, and the commitment to finally address systemic racism. So, for all the obstacles Amanda may have seen or experienced in her long career in public service, she believes it is time for the barriers to change.

Damian Rivera
CEO
Association of Latino Professionals for America, Inc. (ALPFA)

> Equity of opportunity is not the same as equity of responsibility. With increased ability comes increased responsibility. And let there be no doubt the Latino community has amazing abilities, which means we have significant responsibility.
>
> – Damian Rivera

"Do you see that guy over there?" his father asked him in the middle of his abuelo's memorial service. "Yes, Dad, I see him," Damian replied. The man didn't look special to him; he was Latino just like him, with a mustache and beard, dressed in jeans and a black leather jacket. Then his dad asked him, "Do you know what he does?" His dad continued, "He's an engineer. An electrical engineer. Do you know what that means?" Damian thought and replied, "I guess he is like an electrician, so he does electrical work?" "No," his Dad responded, "He does know that stuff but as an electrical engineer he is the one that needs to sign off on permits before new buildings can open up or before people can expand on their properties. He has a lot of power in that position. That's what you want to do in college, you want to be an engineer."

Throughout his life his parents taught him it was okay to dream of doing the impossible things. And how his dad passed along one possible dream to consider. It's funny how when you look back on your life you can see the dots connecting. And even more so when you realize just how smart your parents were in placing you in a position to be able to achieve your biggest dreams. Throughout his life, Damian's parents, David and Doris Rivera, and his brother, Dr. David Rivera Jr., were the foundations by which he was able to achieve his dreams. His father was a college graduate and studied criminal justice, and his mother, although she didn't finish college, is a brilliant collaborator and learner whose life has been dedicated to giving back to the community through nonprofit work. When Damian thinks about growing up in Harlem, New York, the three biggest obstacles to achieving his aspirations were the knowledge gap, the access gap, and what he calls the "risk tolerance gap."

First was the *knowledge gap*. And Damian wants to be very clear as to what he means by "knowledge gap." This is not a capability gap. The issue has never been nor will it ever be that he or anyone else in the Latino community has a capability gap. To the contrary, by every measure of capability the Latino community excels. This is about knowledge of the opportunities. If his father had not opened up his eyes to what it meant to be an engineer, he would never have considered a technology degree in college. Knowing and seeing someone that looked like him as an engineer made it easy for him to picture himself in that space; a lot of people use the phrase "If you can see it, you can be it" (Ad Astra Media's motto). A proof point of this is that he also wanted to be a lawyer. But he didn't see any Latino lawyers in his neighborhood and so he never truly considered that as a career choice.

The second obstacle is *access*. This can be access to information, access to tools, or access to a network of people that can help you along the way. This is another area where Damian was extremely fortunate early in life. His parents put a computer in front of him when he was about seven years old, in 1982: a Commadore Vic 20 computer. They enrolled his brother in Lotus 1-2-3 classes and enrolled him in an after-school and summer program called The Upward Fund. During the summer, this organization had a computer day camp where they were taught programming as well as dining etiquette, preparing them to feel confident when they would one day be in a corporate setting.

Knowledge and access are required but not sufficient. It's important to know where and how to apply your knowledge and access. Although Damian was not consciously aware of this fact until fairly recently, his tolerance for risk was extremely low. He would usually take the fairly safe route. Go to college, take the steady job, continue to perform in the job, and continue to progress. There was nothing wrong with that path but he never really evaluated other options that may have been slightly more risky but would have come with more reward. Looking back, Damian states, "I don't regret a thing." He made it to be one of the top employees as a managing director at an established global company, Accenture. But if he could speak to his younger self he definitely would have encouraged him to pause and consider "What do you plan to do?" more often. And he would have encouraged his younger self to take more risks, earlier.

His father helped him with this later in life when he had an opportunity to take on a role that had the potential to get him to the position of managing director, but at the same time it was an extremely risky role. His father gave him some great words that he takes with him to this day. He said, "What's the worst that can happen? Worst case you can lose your job? Remember, we have been through worse, you'll be okay." He gave him the strength to push to a whole new level of risk tolerance that has resulted in truly living his life to the fullest to this day.

The digital divide is narrowing dramatically within the Latino community. Although there are still issues with respect to internet access in many communities, we are seeing the Latino community persevering, adapting, and finding ways to connect. A report from Nielsen in March 2020 showed that 98 percent of Latino households have a smartphone as compared to 93 percent of the general population and are spending approximately 30-plus hours per week on the smartphone.

The first thing he believes we need to do is to control what we can control as a community. By this, he means identifying opportunities to collaborate more efficiently as a Latino community across the country. There are a myriad of resources that we have as a community, from nonprofit organizations like ALPFA to educational institutions like the many HSI's, Es Tiempo, and Ad Astra Media. In addition, the growing number of Latino college graduates over the past few decades has created success stories across the globe and given risen to a strong group of Latino mentors and sponsors for the upcoming generation. If we mobilize our resources more efficiently as a group, we will be able to bridge the divide more effectively. In parallel, as we organize and collaborate we will see that we will have more power as a group and therefore be able to better push for the changes needed within social, political, and corporate arenas. One example of this is the work being done by Esther Aguilera, CEO of LCDA, who is building a coalition of Latino organizations to push for more Latinos to be appointed to boards and seeing success through those efforts. We are also seeing the same in the political arena with Nathalie Reyes, president and CEO of Latino Victory, helping to get more Latinos to run for political office. And I will also put my own organization in there as well. ALPFA is doing amazing things to educate and mobilize corporate professionals, helping them with the professional development and connections needed to navigate the corporate world and have a seat in that board room.

The answer to how we bridge the divide and create space in the room is a combination of controlling what we can control as a community while engaging in all aspects of life that have created the divide in the first place – from government policies to corporate boardrooms.

Damien has been working as an executive for a great organization that provides professional encouragement. So how do we help more Latinx succeed postcollege? How do you promote diversity, equity, and inclusion, especially in the digital age?

Damien responds: First, we have to live the values that we expect others to implement. Just like any other company we need to have processes and policies in place to ensure we live up to our values of diversity, equity, and inclusivity. It can be something as simple as the phrase we use when we describe ALPFA: "We are Latino focused, but not Latino exclusive, we welcome everyone." The team nationally is extremely diverse, and you see the same thing with the professional and student chapters.

Second, enterprises have to serve their members and corporate partners. One of the keys to success has been how they have engaged in a wholistic approach to development. They expanded out to include six key areas of development: Business Masters, Professional EQ, Wealth Creation, Health and Wellness, Community Engagement, and Xtrapreneurship™. Within each of these areas they engage in discussions around personal growth as well as the hurdles to achieving the growth. The hurdles can range from things you can control, such as mindset, to things that may be out of your explicit control but that you can influence, such as workplace unconscious biases.

Through last year most of their programs were done in person or through webinars, but in August 2021 they launched a completely new learning, development, and engagement platform that he believes will further push the conversation. This platform is a cornerstone of making ALPFA a true digital nonprofit that will reach the Latino community at scale. They have seen the research that 98 percent of Latino homes have access to smartphones. At the same time, enterprises should know one of the biggest challenges to getting equal opportunities and being included is just the knowledge of the opportunity and access to it. This new platform will provide both to anyone who joins. At the same time, it will create the ability to provide engagement between corporations and the community in a way that will improve the discussions in the workplace between their own employees with the goal of those discussions translating to improved policies and practices.

Damien is not a big believer in "best practices," and he proposes that what works well in one place may *not* in another. Best practices in theory come from a lot of places having successfully used them and the belief is that the practice is the right thing to do everywhere. However, best practices don't consider maximum potential. For example, someone could observe a 10 percent improvement in productivity from a specific supply chain process. The process is the best practice and therefore the 10 percent must be the best result. But they wouldn't have considered that maybe if they applied different processes, they could have reached a 20 percent or even 50 percent improvement. Also consider the algorithms that have been trained that the best practice is to hire from Harvard and Columbia because it looks like all the members of the senior executive team come from there, and therefore it must mean they have the best people. That then ties into the AI/ML (artificial intelligence and machine learning) issues that we will have. Training to follow best practices can be a slippery slope. As we consider how to promote leading practices and evaluate for effectiveness, we need to focus less on specific practices and more on the desired outcomes and the processes for ongoing implementation and testing of effectiveness so that each institution can reach its highest potential based on the demographics of the community being served. For example, if the academic setting is a commuter school (i.e., a school where most students do not live on campus) the needs will be different from those for a school where the majority of students live on campus. As a Latino community we need to be involved with our school districts. Starting in elementary school up through college level we need to have more Latinos on school boards and in decision-making positions (i.e., deans, presidents, etc.). This requires deliberate collaboration among various organizations to put together a team to make a difference, for example, collaboration between associations and groups who know Latinos in the community who might be good candidates for school positions. This could lead to work with another group who knows how to prepare someone to run for an elected position. Or use the Latino network to identify someone who is qualified for a college board appointment. The power of the Latino network in getting qualified individuals into these positions will be critical, especially as schools begin to pivot to truly digital learning institutions where AI and ML capabilities will become more prevalent. We need to be in those rooms when the design decisions are made on how the new capabilities will be implemented.

We need to meet them where they are at. While Damien tries to stay away from generalizations, he leans into this one: Latino families are passionate about their children's education. His parents were for him and his brother, and the parents of ALPFA students are the same way. The great news is that studies show the Latino community has a growing rate in college enrollment in the country.

We see that Latino households are 98 percent smartphone enabled, and that Latinos are staying connected through podcasts, smart speakers, and radio shows. So we need to make sure that we are providing the information on how parents can best engage through these means. We need to create more podcasts and develop more voice-enabled skills in Spanish and English. One thing we are doing in ALPFA is creating a learning path for parents of ALPFA students, targeted at first-generation-student parents. It will give the parents insight into what their child may be experiencing in school and how they can best help. This information will be in Spanish as well as English.

Mary Ann Gomez Orta
President and CEO
Congressional Hispanic Leadership Institute (CHLI)

> Diverse points of view create exponentially better results for all. I didn't include it's easy or provides for a quick resolution. I very much appreciate that inviting others to share their expertise and viewpoints adds time and possibly additional actions to a plan, project, or policy.
>
> – Mary Ann Gomez Orta

Mary Ann Gomez Orta is a first-generation American of Mexican heritage. She is the first of five children born and raised in a farmworker camp 45 minutes away from what she calls "civilization," also known as Stockton, California. Her family was poor in finances and rich in traditional values.

Her father, Leonides Gomez, came to the United States from Michoacan, Mexico, in the Bracero Program. Her mom, Margaret Garcia, was born in Brownsville, Texas. They met while working in the fields of Chico, California.

Mary Ann is proud that all five siblings have college degrees. Mary Ann considers that the most significant accomplishment of her parents, who completed third grade, was making sure school was a priority for their children. Her dad used to say that, no matter what happens, no one can take away your education.

Mary Ann grew up speaking Spanish, watching shows on Univision, and dancing to American Bandstand. "I only had access to ABC, NBC, CBS, and Univision. The TV was my primary English language and American culture teacher." Through that screen, she learned about other cultures, countries, languages, and religions. It filled her mind with possibilities.

While sorting potatoes in the packing shed, her mom learned about the University of the Pacific. Her comrades bragged about their daughters going there, so that became her mother's ambition about where Mary Ann was going, too.

Everything at the university was new to her – course topics, time management, loans, and working part-time on campus. And the majority of her classmates were white, from higher socioeconomic beginnings. Her struggle was real. She received a letter she was on academic probation after her first semester. Upset and with a sense of obligation to her family, to not let them down, she asked for help. She was able to get through college with the support of person by the name of Allison Dumas with the Community Involvement Program. It also sparked a new drive in her. "I focused on graduating in front of my family."

Since college graduation, she has mentored many students. She shares her story and encourages them to ask questions and ask for help.

Her personal experience on the digital divide is based on growing up in a farmworker camp. Whenever she would learn about new services, opportunities, or innovations, she would always ask herself, "Will children in farmworker camps have access to this? Will their schools offer it? Will their parents be able to afford it?"

What most children learn, are exposed to in life, or experience beyond what is in the home is through school. If they have access to digital assets at school, it does not matter what their parents can afford. Innovations supply opportunities and possibilities for equitable academic excellence.

Imagine elementary school boards, community college and university presidents, nonprofit and private sector leaders creating local task forces to design equitable digital solutions, to challenge leaders to be solution creators, not just problem solvers. If a decision-making table doesn't exist, start one and decide who you want in those seats. A country's most potent natural resource is its people. If the United States is committed to being a global leader, digital resources must be a funding priority.

The Congressional Hispanic Leadership Institute's (CHLI's) vision is advancing the Hispanic community's diversity of thought. The board of directors is a diverse group of Republican and Democratic members of Congress and corporate executives of different races, ethnic and socioeconomic backgrounds, academic disciplines, and industries.

Diversity, equity, and Hispanic inclusion have always been at the core of CHLI. Before you can promote any concept, you have to invite people to join in the dialogue. As CHLI's CEO, Mary Ann has invited non-Hispanics to be part of their programs. She believes that Hispanics, Latinos, or Latinx want to be invited, hired, promoted, and celebrated; she believes we start by inviting non-Hispanics to our organizations, programs, and social occasions. How else are we to learn from each other? It's not about us or them or others. To succeed, it's about all of us supporting each other.

The foundation of empowerment is investment. Through the CHLI leadership, programs, and alumni activities, Congressional members invest in each other, interns, people, and organizations that support Hispanics. Mary Ann mentions that the most significant investments are in college students. They show them the power of diversity of thought, inclusion, individual and family pride, public service, and servant leadership.

Mary Ann encourages Hispanics/Latinos/Latinx to start by getting involved in a nonprofit at the local level that has a personal meaning to you. Sharpen your skills by practicing good governance, business basics, public relations, and policy. The skills one develops by serving on a nonprofit committee or board flow into other aspects of one's life purpose and day job.

Mary Ann would not be where she is today had she not taken the time to serve on a committee for the American Heart Association (AHA) in Sacramento in 1991. She chose the AHA because she had a brother who died of heart disease when he was only three years old. She learned about committee consensus, media relations, project management, event logistics, networking, and crisis communications. The added value? She also sharpened her advocacy voice.

One of the main obstacles to succeeding in nonprofits is imposter syndrome. It can be challenging to be positive and focus on the work, when most of our lives, we have been the recipients of discrimination and racial or ethnic bias. Mentorship, sponsorship, supportive networks, and life coaching are all ways to help realign goals. Like in any other sector, there may not be many of us at the top levels or even on the second-tier level, but please do not let that stop you from going for it. Reach out for guidance. Maybe the seat is waiting for you!

Antonio Flores, PhD
President
Hispanic Association of Colleges and Universities (HACU)

> Set a worthy purpose for your life and strive to achieve it as if your life depends on it, because it would.
>
> —Antonio Flores

Antonio Flores grew up in a very small and remote rural community in Jalisco, Mexico. The highest level of education available there was fifth grade, which was 150 percent higher than when his parents were young (second grade), and as such he became a first-generation elementary school graduate. When a family of teachers that had been in his home community for some years was transferred to the city of Chapala they spoke to Antonio's parents and offered to take him with them. They believed he could further his education and finish sixth grade there. His parents agreed. This was a life-changing experience for him.

After high school, he went to college to get a degree in education and teacher certification. He taught elementary school for 18 months. While he was working, he went back to college to study for a degree in business administration. The main obstacles to his success in college were the lack of money and a dearth of support networks.

In 1972, at age 25, he emigrated to the United States with the benefit of having a college education but without English proficiency. However, his collegiate experience helped him learn the new language rather rapidly. Two years later, he was admitted to a master's degree program, which he completed in three years while working at a college in Michigan. Years later, he enrolled in a PhD program at the University of Michigan. Every step of the way, he was fortunate to have been mentored and supported by great teachers, colleagues, and friends.

Also, he was able to combine his professional work with his graduate studies. What he was learning he could simultaneously apply to his work as some of his main career challenges were closely related to his studies. This made for his most helpful way of improving in his professional performance while also bringing real situations into his academic endeavors. It was a win-win arrangement, which also helped him to advance professionally rather swiftly. This symbiotic approach has become part and parcel of his work everywhere, including HACU.

As such, his management style includes a heavy dose of continuous teaching and learning: "I share with my reports as much as possible what may be relevant to their own and our team's challenges, but also to seek their input in making important decisions. And they always try to avail themselves of the most current and pertinent information to reach sound conclusions." It is a teaching and learning process grounded in HACU's mission and reality. His college and graduate education armed him with the tools to succeed as president and CEO of this great organization.

The digital divide is a manifestation of the deep inequality that prevails in our society. Those on the upper rungs of the socioeconomic ladder have the most access to broadband connectivity and advanced technology. Those at the bottom have neither. But higher education is the great equalizer and is more accessible and affordable for our emerging generations, even though it is still much more challenging for middle- and lower-income students to get a college education than for those who are better off. Hispanic-Serving Institutions (HSIs) are their community's engine for upward mobility. Higher education degrees are our ticket to leadership positions in society, whether corporate, civic, professional, technical, and so on.

The Hispanic Association of Colleges and Universities (HACU) advocates for greater government investments in HSIs and increased support from the private sector and develops and replicates programs and best practices in the education of Hispanics/Latinx. These efforts along with the support of our membership and partners create more and better higher education opportunities for underserved populations. HSIs not only educate two of every three of the nearly 4 million Hispanic college students, but also serve nearly one of every five African Americans and a plurality of Native Americans and Asian Americans in U.S. higher education, as well as a sizeable number of non-Hispanic whites. Their diverse student population of 6.5 million strong makes HSIs a microcosm of twenty-first-century America. They at HACU are proud to be the voice of HSIs and of their crucial role in educating and training the national workforce for the high technology, high skills, and high critical thinking acumen required for America to remain competitive in the global economy.

The Latino community's best hope is a strong and thriving HSIs cohort, particularly in STEM fields. The 539 HSIs that HACU represents today may be over 600 in a couple of years as they grow by 26–30 per year. However, federal funding to strengthen and expand their capacity has not been growing concurrently. This has created a major inequity that continues to widen with each passing year. They need the national Hispanic community to engage with HACU in persuading the U.S. Congress and the administration to invest fairly in HSIs for the good of the entire country. They also need their help to scale up and institutionalize HACU's initiative to increase substantive collaboration between HSIs and PK–12 schools with large enrollments of Latino and other underserved populations.

PK–12 schools and HSIs need to revamp their outreach and engagement strategies for greater and better parental involvement in their children's education. Their staffing and faculty resources need to reflect the demographics of the families they serve, including competent bilingual/bicultural professionals. Providing access to informal bilingual educator content to augment formal curricula is also vital. Ad Astra Media has free and ready access to this type of content. With this foundation, they could develop new curricular content and materials that would allow them to engage parents as partners in the education of their children. Parents would need to be trained on how to use community resources and the home environment for improved learning and student outcomes, especially parents of limited-English proficiency who are unfamiliar with the educational system. Engaged parents can be the key to their children's educational success.

Francisco Jiménez, PhD
Professor Emeritus
Santa Clara University

> Work hard, respect others, maintain hope and faith, be proud of whom you are and from where you come, and never compromise your integrity.
>
> —Francisco Jiménez

From the time he was 4 until he was 14 years old, Francisco Jiménez's family moved from place to place, following seasonal crops throughout California's Central Valley to earn a living. During that time, they lived in farm labor camps, often in tents or old garages. They finally settled permanently in Bonetti Ranch, a migrant labor camp in Santa Maria, California. His father could not continue working in the fields because of severe back problems. Consequently, his older brother and he worked as janitors 35 hours a week to support their family while still attending school. He studied late into the night after work, seven days a week. In spite of these difficulties, he graduated from high school with honors and received several local scholarships that covered the expenses of his first year at Santa Clara University (SCU). His younger brother, who was a freshman in high school at the time, took over his janitorial job so he could attend college. He was the first in his family to pursue higher education.

Through his writing, public service, and teaching, he promotes diversity and inclusion. He wrote *The Circuit: Stories from the Life of a Migrant Child* (*Cajas de cartón*), *Breaking Through* (*Senderos fronterizos*), *Reaching Out* (*Más allá de mí*), *Taking Hold* (*La Mariposa*), and *The Christmas Gift/El regalo de Navidad* to chronicle part of his family's history but also, more importantly, to document the experiences of a large sector of our society that has been frequently ignored. Through his writing he hopes to give readers an insight into the lives of migrant farm workers, whose noble and back-breaking labor of picking fruits and vegetables puts food on our tables. Their courage, struggles, and hopes and dreams for a better life for their children and their children's children give meaning to the term "American dream." Their story is an important and integral part of the American story.

Through his roles with the Modern Language Association (MLA), he created an ongoing discussion group on Chicano literature to develop a more inclusive literary canon so that the students may see their stories represented as part of the American narrative. As cofounder and coeditor of *The Bilingual Review/La revista bilingue*, later the Bilingual Press, he has played a role in giving access to Latinx writers whose high-quality works are often not accepted by mainstream publishers.

He was appointed to the California Commission on Teacher Credentialing by then California Governor Jerry

Brown, serving as chair for 2 of his 10 years of service. (The Commission is the state agency responsible for establishing credential requirements for all teachers and administrators in California public schools.) During his tenure on the Commission, he strongly supported bilingual education and the continuation and expansion of the requirement that all teachers, during their training, receive instruction that generates awareness of linguistic and cultural diversity. Likewise, during his 6-year tenure on the Western Association Accrediting Commission for Senior Colleges and Universities (WASC) he advocated for integrating diversity in the nine standards used for accrediting colleges and universities in California, Hawaii, and Guam.

As a professor and administrator at Santa Clara, he helped create a community-based learning program, which currently engages more than 1,100 students – almost a quarter of the undergraduate population – each year in service-learning placements throughout the Silicon Valley region. He also worked to establish the University's Ethnic Studies Program and the Eastside Future Teachers Project, which provides college preparatory mentoring and, after college admission, scholarships for approximately 30 East San José high school students interested in pursuing teaching careers. As an associate vice president for academic affairs, he administered an "Excellence through Diversity" grant for $1 million from the James Irvine Foundation. The purpose of the grant was to engage all professors in the different disciplines in teaching, research, and service that enhanced ethnic and racial diversity at SCU. Dr. Jimenez advocates for multicultural education at SCU and elsewhere to ensure that students of different ethnic and socioeconomic backgrounds can appreciate the perspectives of all kinds of people.

As a public speaker, he is frequently invited by county offices of education, school districts, libraries, migrant programs, and community reading programs to make presentations. Oftentimes, he has spent a week in residence visiting six or seven schools in a county prior to holding a community-wide presentation. In addition, he has collaborated with the PEN International Foundation to facilitate extended visits to rural Oregon and Florida and continues to appear at benefits for nonprofit educational organizations.

His hope is that his writing, teaching, and public service have helped create a more inclusive, compassionate, and humane society.

Based on his traumatic experience of failing first grade because he did not know English, he believes Latinos in educational positions can and should promote equity and equality in education. Professors in teacher education programs, for example, can prepare teachers to value the linguistic and cultural assets of all their students and create culturally relevant curricula for language-minority students. The foundational goal of Ad Astra Media was to create culturally appropriate informal science content to teach and inspire individuals from underserved communities and grant access to that content to schools and enterprises. Latinos serving on school boards can pressure state boards of education to include early childhood education mandates for providing language support services for preschool ELL (English language learners) students. They can also implement bilingual programs that maintain and develop both the native language and English.

His parents' involvement in his formal education was limited because they did not speak English and, since they were never able to attend school, they were not familiar with school environments. However, they taught their children the important lessons about life—the values faith and hope, respect, hard work, and perseverance. Nevertheless, he believes that his parents would have been able to be more engaged in his education if the school system had offered them more support. As such, there are various things that can be done to improve parent participation in their children's education: (a) communicate with parents in ways that show them respect and appreciation; (b) create a warm, safe, and inviting environment for them so that they feel welcomed; (c) inform them about the benefits of helping their children to maintain their native language and culture; (d) inform them about their rights and the policies of the school system; (e) provide them with language support and translation if they are non-English speakers; (f) acknowledge and communicate to them the important role they play in the home and in the school for their children to experience and achieve greater gains and academic success; (g) establish an outreach program designed to develop relationships with Latino families; (h) create informal STEM content to inspire future generations of innovators and entrepreneurs. Listen to their concerns, needs, interest areas, and learn about assets and resources within their community.

He and his family lived in a small rural village in the northern part of Jalisco, Mexico, and when he was four years old, they crossed the United States–Mexican border without documentation to escape their poverty and to seek a new and better life. For the next nine years, they moved from place to place following seasonal crops to make a living. At the age of six, he began to work in the fields alongside his parents and older brother, to help make ends meet. During that time, he yearned for stability, for a place to call his own. His desire for a permanent home came, in large part, out of his wish to attend school without interruption. He disliked missing two and a half months of school every year and finding himself way behind in his studies. He enjoyed learning even though school was difficult for him, especially English class. He found a sense of stability and permanence in education, in learning – whatever he learned in school and on his own, that knowledge went with him no matter how many times he moved. It was his to have and to hold.

When he was in the eighth grade, they were deported back to Mexico. Later, he returned to the United States legally, thanks to a Japanese sharecropper for whom he picked strawberries. The sharecropper loaned them money and sponsored them. It was at this time that they settled permanently in Bonetti Ranch, a migrant labor camp in Santa Maria, California. His first year at Santa Clara University was challenging. He felt torn between his responsibilities as a student and his sense of duty to his family. He had self-doubt about being capable of succeeding academically and had a difficult time adjusting to an environment that was different from the community in which he was raised. But he quickly discovered that his migrant experiences were both an obstacle and a blessing. They were an obstacle to the extent that he did not have the social, economic, and educational experiences that some of my classmates enjoyed. However, they were a blessing because they served as a constant reminder of how fortunate he was to be in college. Those experiences convinced him that he should do everything within his power to forge ahead in his studies and not give up. He used those experiences that initially pulled him down to boost himself up. Whenever he felt discouraged, he would jot down recollections about his childhood and prayed to the Virgen de Guadalupe. For the next three years, he received full tuition scholarships from Santa Clara and free room and board in exchange for being a resident assistant. He also worked in the language lab, assisted a professor in her research, and tutored students in Spanish at Bellarmine High School. In 1966, when he was a senior at SCU, he joined César Chávez in the march to Sacramento. As a result of that transformative experience, he pledged to use his education to help alleviate the plight of farm workers.

After graduating from Santa Clara University, he received a Woodrow Wilson Fellowship to attend Columbia University where he received a master's degree and PhD in Latin American literature with emphasis on Mexican literature and culture. His education gave him the context for understanding social injustice, and his childhood experiences gave him the courage and drive to help create a more inclusive and just society through his teaching, public service, and writing.

Based on his educational experiences, his advice to students seeking higher education is to believe in themselves, be confident of their talents and abilities, stay true to their goals, meet challenges with courage and faith, and ask for help when needed. He could have never succeeded in college without the help and guidance he received from his professors.

He believes that the Latino community has the talent and expertise to establish Latino colleges and universities. However, the financial resources to realize that goal are a huge challenge. Several years ago, Roberto Cruz founded National Hispanic University in San José, California. It offered degrees in several disciplines, focusing on preparing bilingual teachers. It struggled financially for several years. Eventually, a for-profit organization took it over, but it too failed due to lack of capital. The campus is now Roberto Cruz Leadership Academy High School, which aptly prepares students for college.

Angel Navarro, JD
Attorney at Law
Law Office of Angel Navarro

GANAS is all you need.

— Jaime Escalante

Angel Navarro was born in East Los Angeles. He spent formative years from (ages 4–10) in Mexico with his father's family. Angel returned to the United States in 1974 at age 10 to live with his mother and two older siblings. He and his siblings attended East Los Angeles schools. He is a first-generation college graduate and the only attorney ever in his entire family. His older sister and older brother both attended and graduated from four-year colleges. His mother did not have money to pay for college. They relied on student loans, grants, and scholarships. College and law school were both difficult. Coming out of ELA (Garfield High School), he began to learn to speak English at age 10, which proved to be challenging. Law school was particularly difficult for him (UCLA Law class of 1990).

The one teacher Angel remembers that got him through all of this was the iconic teacher Mr. Escalante. Jaime Escalante continues to have a positive influence in his life. He did not know it at the time, but he was probably the most inspirational teacher he ever had. He was part of his AP Calculus class in 1982–1983. Angel's class was the class that followed the infamous class of 1982 that was accused of cheating. He can recall that during his senior year at Garfield High School there was constant media attention and TV crews were routinely in his classroom. They had no idea why and Mr. Escalante never told them why. They all knew it had taken place in 1982 but he purposely shielded them from any media scrutiny. He had taken other AP exams prior to the AP Calculus and he was familiar with the process. Typically, their AP teacher would give them an exam and he or she would monitor them to make sure that they completed the exam in the allotted time. When Angel took the AP Calculus exam in May of 1983, he took the exam in the library and Mr. Escalante was not in the room with them. Angel still remembers that he hugged each one of them as they left the classroom and they headed to the library. At the library, there were some people they had never met before. They were apparently monitors from the Educational Testing Center from Princeton, New Jersey, who had been sent to make sure that they were not cheating. This made him very angry. Angel could only imagine now how horrible Mr. Escalante must have felt knowing that these people still could not believe that a bunch of Brown students were outperforming most other students in this very difficult exam. As it turned out, 31 out of 33 of his classmates passed the AP Calculus exam in 1983. They showed those people from New Jersey they were not cheating.

The greatest lesson Angel learned from Mr. Escalante was to never give up. He always told them they were the best. He can still hear his voice saying things like: "You can do it, kid," "You are the best," "Don't let anyone ever tell you otherwise." During his years at Occidental College from 1983 to 1987, he would visit him on a regular basis. He was not too happy with him. He wanted him to study engineering, but he had no interest in studying that field. When Angel told him that he wanted to study law, he did not quite understand that either. He felt that he would have been better off studying engineering as opposed to his double major in political science and economics at Occidental College.

In 1986, Angel was preparing to apply to law school and he was thinking of completing a triple major at Occidental College. He had taken a number of history courses and really wanted to do a major in history as well. His college advisor called him into his office and told him that unfortunately he would not be able to complete a third major for the reason that Occidental College was no longer going to be giving him college credit for his AP Calculus score. He was angry after he was told that he would have to take Calculus in college. He had not taken any math classes at Oxy since he had been told that his AP Calculus score was enough to meet the college math requirements. In any event, Angel went back to his high school and talked to Mr. Escalante. He assured him that he was the best and that he should take the college calculus class and show the people at Occidental College just how smart Escalante's kids really were.

Here is a true story: In the fall of 1986, during his first quarter of Angel's senior year at Occidental College, he took calculus with a group of mostly pre-med students. He was not happy to be in the class since this was preventing him from completing a senior thesis in history and he would not be able to graduate from Occidental College with a triple major. Over the course of the next 10 weeks he received 100 percent in every test and quiz. The final exam was supposed to take three hours to complete. He completed the exam in one hour and gave it to the math professor and told her to use his exam as the key to grade the other exams. She stopped the test and told the entire class that it had been an honor having one of Jaime Escalante's AP Calculus students in her class. This is the influence that Mr. Escalante had on Angel.

He worked as a federal public defender for 18 years (1992–2010). He has been working independently since January of 2010. He is a member of the Criminal Justice Act panel and will continue to represent indigent defendants. He also represents persons in privately retained cases. He enjoys the independence of being his own boss.

The law lacks diversity. Things have not changed much since he became an attorney. The number of attorneys who are people of color is very small. He is always available to mentor and encourage as many people of color to become attorneys.

Angel believes that we need people of color in positions of power to change the narrative. He emphasizes the need for connections, capital, and vision, among other factors.

David Lopez, PhD
Board Member
Silicon Valley Community Foundation

The end of all education should surely be service to others.

– César Chávez

David was born and raised in Albuquerque, New Mexico, and was a first-generation college student. He was the second in his immediate family to attend and graduate from college and receive a Bachelors of Arts degree. As an academically underprepared student, he fortunately qualified and participated in a program at the University of New Mexico (UNM) that provided intensive, personal, and academic support and counseling. He also qualified to participate in a four-year undergraduate work-study program that exposed him to the field of education and provided him access to numerous dynamic and supportive mentors. The mentoring and intensive academic and personal support (at the undergraduate and graduate levels) were keys to his success. Mentors continued to play a significant role in his growth and development in his subsequent professional experiences as a teacher, college professor, and university president.

Silicon Valley is a leading economic and innovation engine well known across the globe, yet when it comes to wealth, economic, educational, and technological disparities the gap is one of the most significant in this area. It is in many ways the tale of two Silicon Valleys. In the heart of Silicon Valley there are particular zip codes where an overwhelming majority of people live in extreme poverty. These communities, mostly people of color, painfully struggle every day with the high costs of housing, food, transportation, healthcare, childcare, and education. Ironically, many of these low-income individuals are classified as "essential workers" and are necessary to the functioning of Silicon Valley; yet they find it exceedingly difficult to live and thrive here. The overwhelming majority are not positioned or prepared to compete for higher paying jobs, especially high-tech industry jobs. Joint Venture Silicon Valley in their 2019 Silicon Valley Index reported that locally only 18 percent of Latinos 25 years and older in Silicon Valley hold a bachelor's degree compared to whites at 62 percent.

For the most part, lower-income people of color are relegated to low-paying jobs and remain undereducated, under-resourced, and undervalued. Leading local employers such as Google, Adobe, Apple, Facebook, and other employers report they can't find enough qualified local talent and continue to recruit heavily from other countries or from other states. In order to address this educational crisis and disparity and not allow people of color to be left behind in the educational, technological, social, and economic advances of this area, we must remove the barriers and prohibitive costs of educational, technological, and socioeconomic opportunities and racism. We must be bold and innovative and strategically invest in ways that level the playing field and have the greatest impact on this historically neglected community. And we must inspire kids of all ages to study and enter STEM careers, as Ad Astra Media states, to show them the magic of STEM.

COVID-19 has also unveiled the deep and underlying inequities, systemic racism, and white supremacy so prevalent and dominant in our communities here and beyond. The impacts are felt the hardest by Black, Brown, and Asian communities, and the appropriate response and recovery period is going to be critical to the success of these communities moving forward. Investments and interventions must address the specific needs, interests, and challenges of people of color.

In this regard, government agencies, technology power-houses, other businesses, and nonprofits have a very unique opportunity in the current environment to strategically col-laborate and invest the financial and human resources needed to address the devastation in our low-income com-munities. What is needed is an eco-system that supports and guides the success of low-income people of color from pre-school to college to career. Silicon Valley tech giants, other business partners, and nonprofits should work together with select educational organizations and establish a Preschool to High-Tech Pipeline Prototype (PHTPP).

The PHTPP would be a bold and innovative initiative to create an aligned educational pipeline prototype for select low-income students and families of color and their schools. A special focus using new and emerging technologies and informal STEM edutainment could help students and their families as they navigate and succeed in pre- and post-secondary education. This prototype would be an intentional vertically aligned educational pipeline commencing with select middle and high schools and eventually adding ele-mentary and preschool feeders.

This prototype would address one of the most nagging and decades-long persistent educational challenges in the region, state, and the nation, the systemic and successful education of low-income people of color. This challenge may seem undo-able and like a "moon shot." But what if a tech company took it on as a moon shot? One such company exists in the Silicon Valley and prides itself in taking on the world's toughest problems and finding solutions. Google X is a specially designed organization within Google that has a mission to address large social problems and find workable solutions.

What if? What if Google X spearheaded the challenge along with others in creating a successful and bold educational and technological prototype for educating low-income people of color? Imagine harnessing Google X's brainpower and other new and emerging technologies and creating a blueprint for success with vulnerable populations right here in the innovation center of the world. What if?

As an educational entrepreneur, David works to create innovative and bold equitable and inclusive solutions in their schools that primarily serve low-income students of color. The following is an example of promoting equity and inclusion using digital technology to help struggling and vulnerable communities. Because of COVID-19, all schools have faced a level of disruption unlike any other time in recent history. California's closure of schools and shelter in place to slow down the spread of COVID-19 have abruptly transitioned teachers and students and their parents to an online instructional format. In these uncertain times, we are not sure about the total impact on our students, families, and their teachers, especially lower-income students of color. Early on in the pandemic, Harvard researcher Raj Chetty found that "Lower income students saw a 60 percent reduction in learning math online and they did not return to previous levels. Higher income students early on experienced a sharp dip in math and within a few weeks the higher income students were back to previous baseline levels or exceeding them."

Even though schools have committed to working hard to provide the best online educational and learning experiences possible, it is fair to say that the educational process and academic success for low-income learners has become much more questionable and challenging.

Educational professionals are challenged in identifying the best and effective online approaches and solutions to help all students, especially the most vulnerable learners. What is known is that low-income learners have limited access to technological hardware, internet accessibility, and knowledge of how to use the technology. These low-income families, especially Latinos and African Americans, have to also cope with the pandemic-related challenges such as the health, economic, and social/emotional tolls experienced by these communities.

As a result of the unrelenting crisis, he has teamed with some educational colleagues and he has launched a small pilot program for "struggling" low-income middle school students not performing up to their potential in this new environment. The goal of the pilot program is to engage, inspire, and motivate middle school students by having them tutor struggling third-grade children in math using a technological online platform.

Early indications are revealing that our middle school students are benefiting from tutoring and mentoring third graders. According to school personnel, the middle school students seem to be exhibiting a better sense of belonging and we are beginning to show improvements in their academic and emotional well-being. Our immediate goal is to demonstrate the positive impact this program can have with middle school students and their third-grade buddies. David hopes to grow the program into the next academic year and scale it throughout the district's middle schools serving low-income students of color. Perhaps the program can grow to serve the increasing number of struggling middle school students throughout Santa Clara County. David believes this is a program that will benefit and provide equity and success for many students of color and their families even way beyond the coronavirus.

California's students of color today make up about 70 percent of the state's student population, while teachers of color are disproportionately at about 30 percent. This challenge is more pronounced for Latinos who, according to the California Department of Education in 2015, comprise approximately 54 percent of the total student K–12 population with only 19 percent Latino teachers. At the national level, the new majority of students of color is over 50 percent, the percentage of teachers who identify as white is 82 percent, and teachers of color comprise about 18 percent. Latino and African American males in the teaching field account for only about 2 percent. Bold initiatives are crucial components to finding replicable solutions for the current educational crisis's impact on students of color, as recent studies exemplify. There are myriad studies that show a direct link between the presence of a teacher of color in the classroom and the subsequent success of students of color.[1]

Districts in California, Wisconsin, Indiana, Alabama, and other states are pledging to employ more teachers who look like their students, according to a recent Brookings Institute

---

[1] A.M. Villegas and J.J. Irvine, "Diversifying the Teaching Force: An Examination of Major Arguments. *Urban Review* 42 (2010), 175–192; A.J. Egalite, "How Family Background Influences Student Achievement," *Education Next* 16, no. 2 (Spring 2016); Anna Egalite, Brian Kisida, and Marcus Winters, "Representation in the Classroom: The Effect on Own-Race Teachers on Student Achievement," *Economics of Education Review* 45, no. 1, (April 2015), ISSN 0272-7757; Denise Marie Ordway, "Minority Teachers: How Students Benefit from Having Teachers from Same Race," May 22, 2017; Ana Maria Villegas and Jacqueline Jordan Irvine, "Diversifying the Teaching Force: An Examination of Major Arguments," *Urban Review: Issues and Ideas in Public Education* 42, no. 3 (September 2010): 175–192.

report from 2016. However, the report also suggests that "significant progress is realistically very slim, even looking forward nearly 50 years, and will require exceptionally ambitious patches to fix the leaky pipeline into the teaching profession." Examples of the "leaky pipeline" in California are how Latino and African Americans students continue to seriously lag well behind their Asian and white peers across the educational spectrum (research conducted by the California Department of Education, 2017). These figures are particularly jarring when comparing their performance against that of their Asian and white counterparts, who hold proficiency rates of 72 percent and 60 percent in reading during the same period, respectively. In mathematics, a recent report entitled "Silicon Valley Competitive and Innovation Project 2016" showed that only 2 out of 10 Latino and African American students in the Silicon Valley region are math proficient at the eighth-grade level, while 8 in 10 Asians and whites are meeting or exceeding the new state standards.

For students of color, the deplorable statistics above and much lower high school and college graduation rates and lack of interest in entering the teaching profession are "the leaks" in the pipeline to produce teachers in California and beyond.

We must address and remedy the glaring opportunity gaps in the state's educational and teacher education pipeline for teachers of color. The most significant leaks in the educational pipeline for students of color, particularly Latinos and African Americans, are graduation rates from high school and college coupled with interest in pursuing a teaching career. We must encourage programs that identify, recruit, encourage, and prepare students of color to become teachers as early as middle school, high school, and at the community college level.

The Latino community as well as other people should demand that institutions of higher education in the region and state work aggressively with the pre-K–12 system to address the challenges of producing much-needed teachers of color. David mentions how we can attract and efficiently fast-track students of color into the teaching profession and increase the available pool of teachers from underserved and low-income communities to serve as role models. A movement or a campaign is also needed to promote, support, and encourage Latinos to become teachers.

5

Technology
Technology Executives

———

Silvina Moshini
Cofounder, President, and Chairwoman
Transparent Business and Executive Producer at
The Unicorn Hunters
  Think BIG; only large companies have BIG impacts.
                                    – Silvina Moshini

SILVINA MOSHINI WAS BORN IN Tandil, a province in Buenos Aires located about four hours from the city. Her family later moved to Buenos Aires, where she obtained her undergraduate degree in Public Relations from UADE University and a degree in marketing from New York University. Later she moved to Texas, where she completed a master's course in communications from the University of Houston. While living in Italy, she completed graduate courses in web communications and social media at the Libera Università di Lingue e Comunicazione and the Università Commerciale Luigi Bocconi, both in Milan.

Silvina is a second-generation college graduate. Her parents always taught her that if she wanted to be independent, she would need to be financially secure. The clearest path to that was to obtain a college degree and, most important, to have the necessary knowledge to pursue her dreams. The greatest challenge was to stay committed to her long-term goal, because when you are young so many roadblocks get in the way – emotional, financial, and even physical. Moving away from her family was a life-changing decision for her. At times, it seemed impossible, but she kept going and today she is very grateful for everyone who supported her – family, professors, and peers.

When the pandemic hit, nearly 40 percent of Latinos did not have broadband internet access at home and 32 percent did not have a computer. The digital divide, which existed long before the crisis, was exacerbated because of it. This is one of the greatest issues of our time, and one that must be addressed by the public sector.

In the era of digital transformation, technology levels the playing field: Students can succeed, businesses can compete, and workers can tap into remote working opportunities no matter where they are based.

Access to the internet should not be viewed as a privilege, but rather a fundamental right.

Governments in advanced economies, such as the United States, have a responsibility to ensure that digital access is provided to all populations – regardless of income or location – and the private sector must continue to show its support with social impact programs that address the needs of underserved populations and advocate for equitable access.

One of the greatest benefits of remote work is that it makes diversity and inclusion the norm. Companies no longer have to hire within a four-mile radius of their headquarters, so they hire the best talent regardless of location, and often this talent is more diverse.

Diversity and inclusion are deeply important to Silvina as a Latinx entrepreneur, because she has experienced firsthand the challenges associated with building a business while being a minority. When the pandemic hit, they donated licenses for start-ups founded by women as well as small and medium businesses (of up to 100 employees) because she wanted to make sure that they too benefited from the digital transformation. In California, they donated $1 million-worth of licenses to local small businesses – the majority of which were Latino-owned because they were disproportionately affected by the crisis.

A great majority of the Latinx community operates small and medium businesses that are the engine of many important economies, from Miami to Los Angeles to Houston. They created a program called FREE25, whose goal is to democratize digitalization. They launched this initiative because Silvina believes that the benefits of digital transformation should not be reserved for big tech companies or multinational corporations. Visit: http://www.transparent-business.com.

Sandra Lopez
Vice President/GM
Intel

Si se puede.

— César Chávez

Sandra Lopez grew up in Foster City, California, which at that time was arguably upper middle class, with the majority of Caucasian descent. As a first-generation American, her greatest obstacle was learning the ropes. Sandra was the first to leave for college and did not have parents who understood the admission process or college living. Given her parents were traditional Mexican-Catholic, the geographical setting of the college became an important criterion in the college selection process. From their perspective, a woman should not be too distant from the family. As such, Sandra identified colleges within the state as she did not want to disappoint her parents. Ultimately, her greatest challenge in college was her parents. They both grew up in a small town in Mexico and exposure to college living was nonexistent. They understood the importance of college, yet how to experience college was always a challenge for them to understand.

The digital divide follows the economic divide. If one does not have the financial means to purchase electronics and/or if the children do not have access to technology at school, they will be forever at a disadvantage. The pandemic punctuated the digital divide with virtual classes. It has seen so many images of kids going to their nearby school to obtain Wi-Fi access that should not happen in a first-world country. Sandra believes the digital divide provides an opportunity for both the public and private sector to work together to address the gap. Sandra's current company has done a lot to give back to the community and provide some communities with access to PCs.

Sandra is a Latina who believes it is her responsibility to help further open the door for the next generation. Thus, she does her best to ensure that in her every action, she has a diversity and inclusion filter. Sandra is an example; if hiring, she starts with a diverse pool of candidates. If Sandra knows there is an introvert in the room, she establishes an environment to ensure their voice is heard. Finally, she continuously evaluates her organization to ensure Intel is addressing pay equity and promotions.

As the Latinx community becomes a growing majority, they have seen their influence in politics. Technology companies must ensure their voices are represented in the algorithms that are being designed and the products and services that are being engineered.

Latinx face similar obstacles across various industries. To overcome them, one must first have understanding. In the technology industry, it must begin with the parents understanding the career path of a technologist. Oftentimes, Latinx parents focus on "known" careers: doctor, lawyer, business. As a result, they can easily influence their child not to pursue a career in technology. As one enters the technology industry, finding one's voice becomes critical; however, in Latinx culture we have been influenced by the concept of *respeto*. How we were conditioned as a child affects us in the corporate world because we are hired to challenge the status quo, have a point of view, and so on. Yet, growing up we are conditioned to obey and do what *abuelita* tells us to do and not to question her.

Understanding the various roles that can exist within technology is integral to success. One does not have to be an engineer to succeed in technology. Latinos can be great marketers, great financers, great people who succeed in technology. One must realize that technology is shaping society and if one is interested in affecting change, then they should seriously consider a career in technology. It begins with curiosity and open-mindedness and allowing one's professional journey to zigzag. Sometimes the unexpected route provides the greatest growth trajectory.

Diana Juarez Madera
Systems Engineer
Aeronautics, Astronautics

> I serve mankind by making dreams come true.
>
>   – Anonymous

Diana Juarez Madera was born and raised in central Mexico. Diana is a first-generation college graduate as her mother did not attend high school and her father did not finish elementary school. Her mother was a stay-at-home mom and her father dedicated to cultivate the land. The lack of light pollution in her humble community allowed her to have a first-row-seat view of the night sky, which touched her deeply. Since she was a little girl she wanted to understand the portion of the universe she was able to see from outside her home, and while growing up she was good at math and science. Growing up, she heard stories about her grandfather promoting education in his extreme-poverty community, where he made every effort to teach children what he had learned through books. She believes those stories motivated her to pursue excellence in the academic setting. Unfortunately, in her remote and rural community, a woman associated with college is scarce, let alone involved in physics and space. That was unheard of! For her future, she was expected to live a more conventional life. She was expected to get married early and stay at home to raise the children. This, however, was not for her. There were moments when she wanted to walk away from conventional norms. She did not feel supported to do things outside the standard for a woman from a rural community in Mexico. To make matters worse, the challenges toward becoming a space professional started at home. Unfortunately, her home environment was very dysfunctional, and her father was affected by alcoholism. More times than not it was very difficult to maintain the motivation, even the meaning of life at all. Moreover, her youngest sister's health problems aggravated the despair. Despite the distress, her mother kept strong, motivating her siblings and her to excel at school. "*La única herencia que les puedo dejar es el estudio,*" her mother constantly stated as part of her encouragement. For the most part the education she received in Mexico was low cost or free, so her mother contributed by preparing food for them and keeping the house clean so they could focus on studying.

There were times when her father offered some motivation when her sadness was at its deepest depths. Although he lacked a much-needed loving tone, she believes he had noble intentions.

After all, it must have been difficult to deal with a daughter who rejected the standard way of life and who threatened to drag him into a future he did not understand. Sadly, others find their escape from such a dysfunctional toxic family nucleus through drugs and poor decisions. Fortunately, all the effort that her mother put into her was the fuel that kept her going, and she is thankful that studying hard became her escape. Diana believes the Latinx society should cultivate interest in science and technology in their daily lives. This highlights the importance of Ad Astra Media, which is seeking to inspire kids to study and enter the STEM fields. Once we are there, the interest in learning something new, such as becoming proficient in digital technologies, can become second nature. Our current lifestyle within an interconnected world makes access to the internet a necessity, not a luxury.

To narrow the digital divide, providing free access to underserved communities is key. Expand the resources allocated for facilities such as public libraries and community centers, and make the Latinx community aware that the resources are free at those locations. Also, schools partnering with government to provide hotspots for every student for home use could help us narrow the digital divide faster.

Once larger-scale access is achieved, members of the Latinx community have to stop being afraid of learning new things and dive into the online world. Diana would encourage them to not give up just because it did not work the first few times. On the point about "How can we be at the decision-making table?" Diana believes that Latinx people came to this country to build a better life. In a sense they felt their own governments failed them back home. Some of those governments cannot get anything done because they don't get serious.

To be at the decision-making table, the Latinx community has to get serious. Latinx immigrants in the United States have the opportunity to get serious. We strongly encourage Latinx community members to not put limits on themselves and to not be influenced by foolish stereotypes and prejudice such as sexism/machismo that blinds fruitful action. Fathers have to embrace their daughters' potential and make sure they let them know they can become anything in life without limits. Diana would encourage members of the Latinx community to not ignore problems and instead tackle them directly to get ahead. See a problem? Work on a solution, don't put it off until later. This is the core of innovation. It takes work. Everything takes work. Nothing is accomplished without work. We as Latinx have to awaken, organize, and go take the power that belongs to us; no one is going to give it to us unless we start taking risks.

The encouragement of someone close to us is the little push we all need to get ahead. That someone can be a mother, a father, an uncle, a friend. When she was a teenager, her uncle and aunt constantly asked her: "*¿Qué vas a estudiar cuando seas grande?*" That simple question made her realize that a career was something to consider in her life and it was of big importance. Diana came to realize that, with the lack of an astronomy career option in Central Mexico, studying physics was going to get her closer to fulfilling her desires. From elementary school she competed in academic contests, and she constantly brought home multiple recognitions and awards. One such award distributed computer systems to top students. This was a game changer as her parents did not have the means to purchase a computer for her that could help her turn in better homework assignments. She believes that her academic discipline and God's favor compensated her during the last year of her undergraduate education when she became the first winner of the John N. Bahcall Award, in honor of his pioneering work in astro-particle physics.

She was in a national competition in Mexico that granted her a summer position at the University of California, Santa Cruz (UCSC) as specialist in the field of astrophysics. She graduated with a BS in physics from Universidad Autonoma de Zacatecas with honors, and later she went on to work toward her MS in physics at San Francisco State University (SFSU) alongside her husband. She graduated with honors from SFSU. Close to graduation, she discovered her passion for rocket science! The daily drive by the San Francisco International Airport made her realize that aerospace engineering was the bridge that would connect her to the exploration of the night sky she had observed as a girl. She then pursued a PhD in aeronautics and astronautics at Stanford University, which offered one of the top programs of the nation in the field.

Her parents were not much involved in her higher education because they did not understand what physics or astronautics was. As a first-generation student, her path in college and graduate school was not easy, since she had to figure out for herself what was the next step to take every time. During the most difficult times at San Francisco State and Stanford, she came across people who cared, friends, certain professors, and people in higher roles such as associate deans of engineering.

Those encounters kept her going as she realized that someone actually cared if she graduated. As Diana mentioned, one must always be willing to learn something new.

Immigrants come to this country with the desire to build a better future. However, the society in this country is dominated by the English language. In order to have access to optimum opportunities offered by this country we could make a bigger effort to become English proficient. Spanish is a beautiful language that we must continue to pass to future generations, but bilingualism and biliteracy can only put us at an advantage. If you are shy about speaking English because you are just starting to learn, don't be afraid to speak, leave your comfort zone and say what you need to say. The right pronunciation will come with practice, practice, practice! Latinx youth have to start populating colleges and universities. Even more so graduate schools, because finishing graduate school becomes "part of the solution." Do not be afraid of graduate school. For certain programs, among them STEM fields, graduate school can get paid for with scholarships and fellowships. That removes the loan borrowing factor. You don't have to be awarded a big fellowship, but you can have multiple smaller fellowships to make ends meet. A higher presence of Latinx members in higher education can be a model for future generations to help them to believe they belong there. Sadly, stereotyping and racism also exist among members of the Latinx community. We must start practicing more equality among ourselves, among women and men, stop the "machismo" culture. Stop thinking of someone else as a less person because of the color of their skin. And do not downplay the achievements of other Latinxs. If we cannot change this mindset, we have lost the battle. Diana believes that we have to be open to build relationships with people from other cultures. Educating youth is a shared responsibility. By opening to the world, the world can open to us. In this way we can build a broader sense of community. Engaging with others on intellectual and emotional levels can help us create opportunities for access and at the same time share responsibility and accountability. Members of the Latinx community must organize to be more involved in advocacy activities and help facilitate such practices.

Make involvement easier for hard-working parents. Diana believes that the constraint that weights the most and impedes the involvement of Spanish-speaking parents in their child's education is long working hours. Legislation should be passed that permits work leave to allow parents the time to attend school activities with their kids. Additionally, community centers could establish sessions to help Spanish-speaking parents learn to access the internet and establish online parent-teacher connections to guide parents on their children's needs and update parents of academic events through social media. However, she also believes that there are special cases in which Spanish-speaking parents are not involved in their child's education because they themselves did not attend school, and do not know how to guide their children. This is vital because parents or family members that show even the smallest interest in one's education could be a driving force for kids and teenagers to achieve greater goals.

Guillermo Diaz
Chief Executive Officer
Kloudspot

Always remember where you came from, to know where you are going.

– Guillermo Diaz

After 20 years of a great career at Cisco, leading the IT, Technology, and Transformation department, Guillermo Diaz mentions it was time to move into a new phase, one that combines what he has built on his foundation and career thus far.

Guillermo wanted to combine his purpose of building that intersection and something that would change the world. Guillermo mentioned that he is leading Kloudspot as CEO to "Inspire Lives – in Real Time," using AI and the power of the network to give people insights, in real time, to make decisions on their next actions – shoppers, employees, and students.

Also, as Chairman of HITEC, he is laser-focused on raising the next generation of Technology Leaders, who happen to be Latino – all the way down to the students at (Cristo Rey San José Jesuit High School, in San José, California). He is also on the board of directors of Blue Shield of California, in the heart of the biggest issue that the world is facing: healthcare.

When Guillermo looks back, he recalls his first glimpse of his platform as a young Navy sailor. He had no concept of diversity because he grew up on the eastside of Pueblo, Colorado, which is a mostly Latino community. Looking back, he realizes this made him a bit sheltered. One day, in a Navy boot-camp inspection, the commander asked him to remove his cover (hat). He took a look at Guillermo's hair, which was just growing back from "the shave," and was slicked back. He said, "How did they let a *cholo* like you in my Navy?"

Guillermo did everything he could to not do something stupid, but in reality that was a powerful moment for him. A moment when he told himself that he would never, ever let anyone tell him what he could or could not do. It created a fire, an inspiration, a determination to "Never allow himself to let color, race, gender, or whatever get in the way of moving myself and others forward. *Adelante.*"

He didn't realize it at the time, but the Navy helped lay the groundwork for his platform. A platform that bridges people and technology.

In addition to inspiring his drive to move forward, Guillermo credits the Navy for his introduction to technology. It's where he learned about an exciting field called telecommunications and networks. The technology experience he gained allowed him to accelerate his career and would ultimately provide him the privilege of becoming an executive leader at one of the greatest technology companies in the world: Cisco.

In the early days of the internet and communications, it became evident that this was a hot area, and Guillermo felt like it was in the right place at the right time. So, a bit of luck – and a lot of *ganas* and passion – helped him find his path.

Along the way, although he loved his job, he knew he had even more to offer. Guillermo asked himself, "Why am I on this earth? How did I end up here, where all this technology is taking off?" The answer came to him over time.

"Always remember where you came from to know where you are going." This phrase stuck with him and now he can share it with others. Guillermo reminds us that our past makes us who we are and creates our foundation. That foundation can be used as a springboard to do new and exciting things that impact the world.

A short time later, he was at a community event for Cisco Conexión where they were giving out backpacks to students – an event he didn't feel he had time for because he was too busy at work. A little boy cried when he gave him a backpack. When he asked why, he replied, "I've never had a backpack before." He had to take a moment. He told himself, "You have to step up here, buddy." It was then he realized that his role wasn't just about work anymore; it was broader. "I now had a clear purpose: to help raise the next generation of leaders – of Hispanic technology leaders."

In the technology industry, the bar seems to be set at 5 percent. If your company has a Hispanic/Latinx demographic of 5 percent, then you're doing pretty well. With Hispanic women the numbers dwindle even more. And that's just not good enough. This is where he believes that he can make an impact and has fully embraced his purpose of raising the next generation of Hispanic technology leaders.

He is very proud of the work being done by the Hispanic IT Executive Council (HITEC) Foundation, which focuses on students in technology. He served as the board chair of the foundation and has worked with incredible people who share his purpose. In 2020, he was blessed to become chairman of the broader HITEC organization, and they are laser-focused on building executive leadership in technology and bridging to the pipeline provided by the HITEC Foundation.

He often has the opportunity to connect with peers and customers, and when he asked them about the biggest impediment to driving a transformation or change, the answer he used to expect was "technology."

Culture is propagated and inspired by the leader, and as leaders we have the opportunity to influence real change.

Leaders have to believe in the vision they set with all their heart. (Leaders wear their heart on their sleeve, to believe in something big.)

More importantly, leaders have to believe in the power of *relationships*. He calls his philosophy ROI, which stands for Relationships Over Issues – something he learned from a great mentor of his. Every day we deal with issues. But just like financial ROI (return on investment), when you invest in relationships, the business and emotional returns from resolving issues can be exponential. So really, ROI equals ROI.

Every year, Guillermo sets the tone for his teams with a word or phrase for the year. This year's phrase is: "Inspire reinvention." He would ask himself every day, "Are you living up to that phrase?" He has driven reinvention in the past, but this year it has a more profound personal meaning. He shifted his role at Cisco and his role in HITEC, so he is resilient in changing his whole mindset. After having been in IT for decades, he is taking the foundation he built to reinvent himself.

Guillermo feels very strongly about leveraging his platform to fulfill his purpose. His hope is that all of you feel the same responsibility to raise the next generation to walk in your shoes someday.

Felicidades!

Jose Hernandez
President and CEO
Tierra Luna Engineering, LLC

Se Vale Soñar en GRANDE – dream BIG.

– Jose Hernandez

Jose Hernandez's story began well before he was born. His father, at age 15, first came to the United States out of economic necessity to work in the only area he knew, which was agriculture. Like many of his fellow Michoacanos from Mexico, he quickly established a routine where he would cross the border without proper documentation and follow the harvest. First he would work two months in Southern California and afterward move to Central California, near Salinas, for another two months, and finally he would move on to the Northern California in the Stockton area, where he would spend five months.

Jose's dad would return to Mexico for three months in the wintertime and the cycle would repeat itself year after year. After turning 18 his father was able to get his documents in order and was free to come and go as he pleased.

His parents were married very young, and his father included his mother in this *corrida,* or nomadic lifestyle, in which they spent nine months in California and three months in Michoacan, Mexico. With marriage came the kids, and Jose is the youngest of four. Where one was born was dictated by the month of birth. Two siblings were born during peak harvest season and thus were born in California, while the two eldest siblings were born in the winter months and thus call Mexico their birthplace.

Going to school was difficult for Jose in the beginning, as he had three different teachers in three different cities in one school year. To make matters worse, the children self-studied in Mexico for three months by taking three months' worth of homework from their teachers. This was not a very conducive environment in which to learn the English language, let alone the lesson plan of the teachers! Things improved when his second-grade teacher paid a visit to his parents and convinced them to leave this nomadic lifestyle. This was when the family began to call Stockton, California, their home. They still went to Mexico every year but their three-month trips shrank to only three weeks centered on the Christmas vacation. It was then when the children's education finally began to gain traction.

Jose's dream of becoming an astronaut was conceived when he was 10 years old. If you can picture a 10-year-old boy kneeling in front of an old black-and-white vacuum-tube television with rabbit-ear antennas watching the very last Apollo mission, well, that was Jose. The Apollo era was when the United States was first sending humans to the moon. When this occurred the family could watch the launch, the landing on the moon, and the astronauts walking in low gravity, ending with the splashdown return to Earth. He was lucky enough to have caught the very last mission of this era, which was the *Apollo 17* mission. Upon seeing and hearing astronaut Eugene Cernan walk on the moon, he knew that this was what he wanted to be! He shared this dream with his father that same evening. Jose recalls that although his father and mother only had third-grade educations, they had the wisdom to empower his dreams and make him believe he could reach it! With this empowerment he set out on his journey to become an astronaut.

The journey was long and arduous. It is not easy for a young boy growing up in a bicultural environment to succeed, particularly a boy living with the great socioeconomic challenges he had. But he forged ahead, and instead of getting distracted with drugs, low-riders, and the way of life in their barrio, Jose focused on his studies. He still assimilated in his neighborhood as he drove around in a slightly lowered 1964 Chevy Impala Super Sport. It was out of necessity that one assimilates so as not to be targeted by neighborhood gang members. Paying for college was another challenge, but through his high school counselor, he got a decent paying job at a cannery that turned tomatoes into ketchup and fruit into canned fruit cocktail. Once graduating from college, he decided to continue his studies and went to pursue his graduate degree. From there he was hired at Lawrence Livermore National Laboratory and, when eligible, immediately began to apply to the NASA Astronaut program. Getting selected was not easy. One has to not let rejection bring you down. Instead one needs to learn from failures so that one can better prepare oneself before making another attempt. Perseverance is another trait he needed: NASA rejected him 11 times before he was finally accepted to the 19th class of astronauts on his 12th attempt.

The digital divide is a phenomenon that especially affects the Latino community. For those of us who take having access to the internet and knowing how to use computers for granted, Jose makes a comparison that perhaps will help you appreciate just how real this divide is. He sees teaching computer literacy as difficult as teaching another language. In other words, if someone came and spoke to you in a language you did not understand, imagine how frustrating it would be if you needed to fill out forms in that particular language. The same occurs with people who have not been around computers or the internet, and yet they are expected to fill forms online, have parent-teacher meetings via Zoom, download the grades of their children, and so on.

The solution? Jose believes greater and more concentrated efforts should be made in offering courses and workshops to people who want to learn. But it does not have to stop there, because resources are also required to close the gap on this great digital divide. Some families simply cannot afford a monthly internet bill, let alone a computer. To solve this problem, he believes computer manufacturers should partner with government and give families that demonstrate the need some basic training, and that service providers should be required to give free access to the internet to these families. Furthermore, community centers should have hot spots and courses on using the computers and internet. In doing so, we can make the Latino community more computer-literate, allowing them to take advantage of online social and medical services.

Isaura S. Gaeta
Vice President, Security Research
Intel Product Assurance and Security Engineering

El derecho ajeno es la paz.

– Isaura S. Gaeta

Isaura S. Gaeta was born in Chicago, Illinois, to a family that lived in a Spanish-speaking barrio. She didn't learn to speak English until she was five years old and her family moved to California. Isaura is between the first and second generation in the United States, but there is some interesting background to her U.S. status. Her father was also born in Chicago in 1930, but soon thereafter, during the Mexican

Repatriation, his family was deported to Jalisco, Mexico. Her father then returned to the United States in his late teens and was a farmworker in Bakersfield until he was drafted into the U.S. Army. Her mother is from Guadalajara, Mexico, and married Isaura's father when he finished his service in the army and they settled in Chicago. Her father learned to be a machinist in the army and then held a blue-collar job in Chicago. Since both of her parents did not finish high school, they strongly encouraged her and her brothers to study and do well in school. Isaura and her older brother are the first generation to go to college within a year of each other. They both received scholarships to study engineering.

Going to college and studying engineering was not originally the plan for both of them. Isaura attended public schools in Santa Clara County, and the system did not encourage Latino kids to prepare for college in those days. Her high school counselor would not allow her to take Drafting and Electronics because "girls don't take those classes," and he scoffed when she told him her desire was to apply to Stanford University. He told her she would never be accepted and that she would be better off applying to the local state university. Luckily, she did not follow his advice and eventually did take the classes she wanted to take and applied and was accepted to Stanford University, where Isaura studied Electrical Engineering.

Studying electrical engineering at Stanford was very difficult, especially since Isaura's high school had not offered Calculus or advanced science courses, so she was experiencing most of the math and science concepts for the very first time. Competing against private school kids who were very well prepared was intimidating and made Isaura feel like she didn't belong. Thankfully, Stanford was just starting to have Chicano student groups, and she joined the pre-engineering group and, together with her peers, they powered through the courses. If she had not had this Latino student community, she doesn't think she would have made it through her first year. In her senior year, Isaura was the president of the pre-engineering group, the Stanford Society of Chicano and Latino Engineers and Scientists – a position that helped her develop her early leadership skills. She stayed at Stanford for her master's degree, also in Electrical Engineering, with a focus on logic design and semiconductor processing.

One of the best decisions she made in graduate school was to focus on her coursework in semiconductor processing. This combination of science, chemistry, physics, electrical engineering, and computer modeling was not only fun to learn but is also the basis for computer chip manufacturing, which is what made Santa Clara Valley become "Silicon Valley." Upon graduation, she started working at Fairchild Semiconductor in Mountain View at an astounding salary of $27,900 per year. Isaura was ready to lean in, but the workplace was not ready for someone like her.

In the early 1980s, the semiconductor industry was still in the wild west days of chip design. Many business decisions were made through wheeling and dealing during cigarette-smoke-filled lunches, and those decisions were mainly in the hands of the white male engineers who dominated the workforce at that time. Imagine that along comes a petite young Latina engineer with Stanford ideas on how to design experiments or write up their technical reports: Isaura either received startled looks or was ignored by her colleagues.

They couldn't ignore her results though, so she managed to power through once again due to perseverance and hard work.

Isaura's secret power during this time is that she spent a lot of time in the wafer fabrication area (the Fab) learning how things worked. Most of the technicians in the Fab were Latino or Filipino, so she bonded with them and learned a lot from them. They would run her experiments with extra care and give her advice on which tools were running the best, which helped her to achieve the best outcomes on these experiments. Although her engineering colleagues had a hard time accepting her, her Fab buddies were her *communidad* and helped her develop the skills that made her a great engineer. One of the little-known Silicon Valley stories is about these amazing technicians who enabled the success of semiconductor companies, and many of these technicians were Latinas!

After two years at Fairchild, Isaura left to go to Intel Corporation, where she was promoted quickly based on her experience developing semiconductor technologies. She has been at Intel for more than 35 years and has worked in multiple sectors of the business.

Growing up in Silicon Valley, she experienced the digital divide, but she truly believed the situation would improve quickly over time. During her generation, there were scholarships and outreach to get more Latinx students to go into engineering. In the early 1980s, they formed the San José Coalition of Latino Engineers and Scientists (CLES) a group of like-minded young professional Latinos from IBM, General Electric, Lockheed, Westinghouse, PG&E, and Intel. They held workshops on engineering and did a lot of activities with students. It seemed at the time that more students were going into engineering than ever before. But then in the late 1980s, with growing demand for computer scientists, many professors joined the industry and left universities unprepared to handle a surge of students. Admission was limited and, ultimately, the number of computer science graduates declined. As the demand was filled by foreign graduates, U.S. students steered away from engineering because the opportunities were limited. The number of scholarships for engineering students reduced, and the number of Latinos going into engineering also declined as a result. Sadly, the interest in engineering careers dwindled, especially in the Latino community.

In the era of the internet and with the allure of entrepreneurial successes of companies like Google and Facebook, technology careers have made a comeback. For the Latino community, it has been difficult to shift gears because preparation for a career in technology starts in middle school. It is important to take the right middle school math and science classes to enable eligibility for college prep classes in high school. Unfortunately, many public schools in predominately Latino neighborhoods don't have enough resources to offer these courses. Many of these gaps are made up for by nonprofit groups focused on education (e.g., the Hispanic Foundation of Silicon Valley) or charter/private schools with a focus on outreach to Latino students, or private sector companies like Ad Astra Media.

What can industry do to help bridge the digital divide? First, it is in the best interest of the technology sector to help improve the educational outcome of the communities where they are located, partnering private sector and nonprofit entities to create specific content to teach appropriate skills training. Not only does this create a future workforce from which to hire, but it also provides a retention incentive for current employees if the community provides a high-quality education for their children. Second, internship opportunities are a win-win employment situation. An intern gains the exposure and skills during an internship, making them a more desirable hire once they graduate. The company that takes on the intern can assess that student's strengths and weaknesses and can train them to be a great fit for their unique needs. With the modest investment of an internship, the company may generate a pipeline of diverse talent.

For companies to see the opportunities that may exist in their own backyard, it is important to have ears and eyes in their surrounding communities. One easy way to do this is by supporting employee resource groups or affinity groups that do outreach in the community. By listening to these employee voices, they can learn specifically where they can have the biggest impact. For example, if awareness of career opportunities is a gap, the company can support employees to visit local schools or universities to talk about careers with students. If the gap is in school resources, the company may offer grants or allow employees to volunteer time to fill these gaps. If every company pitched in a bit, the entire community would benefit, and we could go a long way in closing the digital divide across communities.

Isaura is the Vice President of Security Research in the Product Assurance and Security group at Intel Corporation. She currently leads a team of hackers and they try to break their products before they go into production. Isaura has worked in semiconductor processing, hardware design, and now security research – all which has an under-representation of women and Latinos. She is very motivated to raise awareness and open doors to improve representation in these fields. When they have job openings, they try hard to fill them with diverse individuals. Within her company, she sits on the Executive Diversity Council with their company's CEO, where they advocate for internal and external diversity, inclusion, and equity measures to improve their workplace and the industry. She is an advisor for employee resource groups for Latinos, technical women, LGBTQ, and Latin American–region employees. In addition, she sits on the board of a nonprofit organization dedicated to inspiring community philanthropy and engaging people to invest in the educational achievement in the Hispanic Community.

Isaura states she is not an overnight success. She has gotten to where she is in her career due to hard work and perseverance steadily over three decades. One of her strongest attributes is persistence. She does not give up easily. She can point to several times during her career when opportunities that she was interested in were not offered to her. She remembers one case where her leadership team was considering relocating their group from California to Oregon. The leader of the group went to every manager and asked them specifically if they would make the move and what position they would be interested to take in this new organization. She noticed that he didn't ask her. When she asked him about it, he said, "Oh, you are married and have kids, so I didn't think you would be interested in moving." There were other more subtle snubs where she was not automatically selected for the new project or for upcoming promotions. She is certain many of these were due to unconscious bias where they don't even think of the petite Latina and revert to their "go-to guys" almost by instinct. She had to learn, through trial and error, how to get her voice heard and how to advocate for herself in a way that was acceptable in the workforce. It was difficult, but this is how she progressed.

Isaura can't point to a specific mentor she had during the first two decades of her career, but she did have several allies. These allies could be colleagues who really respected her work and would support her ideas when she spoke up in meetings. The allies were also other female engineers; they were few and far between, so it was a survival skill to have each other's backs and share information on upcoming jobs or individuals to avoid in the workplace. Her allies were also other Latinos (mostly men) either at work or in the professional engineering organizations that she participated in outside of work. Those organizations, such as the Society of Hispanic Professional Engineers (SHPE), for which she was the San José chapter president in the mid-1980s, helped build leadership skills that were completely fungible to the workplace and thus also played a part in her career growth.

More recently, she has had mentors and sponsors in her life. She really values the senior leadership advice they gave her as there were few role models early in her life who attained the level of VP, SVP, or CEO. Learning to navigate corporate America at the highest levels requires a strong support group, mentors, allies, and sponsors.

Growing up, Isaura's father taught her to treat everyone with respect. So, she chose the following quote from Benito

Juarez for her high school yearbook, under her graduation photo, "*El derecho ajeno es la paz.*" She makes it a point to say hello and thank you to all custodial and cafeteria workers at her workplace, as she believes their jobs are just as important as hers.

More recently, Isaura started to use the following acronym to represent her mission – CPU. As a woman in the industry, she focused on building CPUs, the central processing unit or so-called brains of the computer. Her own CPU acronym stands for Commit, Persist, and Unite. Commit to be your best self every day. Persist despite setbacks. And Unite, because you can't get there alone.

6

Abundance
Media and Arts

Jorge Ferraez
President and Publisher
***Latino Leaders* Magazine**
  Include Latino-inspired and -driven content in all these
  platforms. In one word: ownership.
                                                    – Jorge Ferraez

JORGE FERRAEZ WAS BORN IN the city of Merida in Mexico and
grew up in Mexico City. Both his parents got their college
degrees – his mom as a business administrator and his dad as
an architect. On both sides of the family, professional degrees
were common, so it never crossed his mind when he was
growing up that his experience could be the exception. His
obstacles were more on the side of the financial conditions of
his family to be able to support him and his college degree.
He had to work from the very start to pay for his studies.

The best advice he has ever heard on this topic is that we Latinos need to have more ownership of media outlets and content production companies. If we don't have ownership, we will always be asking for our share. The thing is not to have to ask, but to own the media and use it to include Latino inspired and driven content on all these platforms. In one word: ownership.

Jorge is fortunate to be a publisher and the owner of his own publishing company, which has been around for 20 years and has a great recognition and brand equity. His mission statement is to promote Latino leadership across all areas and industries, to showcase the stories of success of Latinos in America, thus highlighting the contributions they are making to our country and society.

In terms of the content, the names, stories, and places are real and alive. These are actual humans and the organizations led by them that are functioning parts of our communities. They exist, and if they exist, it means that others can exist too. They are successful cases that can be reproduced and can occur again. Others can be inspired to make them happen.

Ownership – that's the best way to influence and advance Latinos in media. Unless you own the media, you will always be soliciting an opportunity. Latinos need to start owning or being at least part owners of big media companies. The news media is the fourth power! We need to invest and create our own media and not depend on other media, with interests that won't always be in our favor. Also, the numbers should be good enough to persuade the media giants to start moving the needle for better inclusion of Latinos in their outlets. The 2020 Census should be the biggest trigger for these types of policy changes. Big corporations should start feeling the pressure to expand their outreach for diversity and inclusion in the Hispanic markets very soon.

Manny Ruiz
Cofounder
Brilla Media

> This has varied through the years but the one quote I TRY to remember in the many ups and downs of my life and career is from the Bible: "Let us not become weary in doing good, for at the proper time we will reap a harvest if we do not give up."
>
> – Manny Ruiz

Manny Ruiz was born and raised in a working-class neighborhood in the Little Havana neighborhood of Miami, in a small duplex owned by his maternal grandparents, who raised him. His grandfather Manolo, whom he was named after, came to the United States in 1921 and married Manny's grandmother Margarita in New York City in 1941. His mom was born in Miami in 1948, so he is a second-generation American from his mom's side and the first of that small part of the family to have a college degree.

In terms of academics, he always struggled mightily, especially with math. He went to summer school for math in six and seventh grade and even repeated his entire senior year, largely because he struggled at math. While he was very bad at math, he was actually excellent at logic and arithmetic, he did well in English and especially excelled at journalism, both in high school and college. It was because of journalism and some gutsy work as a student newspaper editor that Manny went to college for free and with some help from Pell Grants, which he qualified for because of his household's very low income.

The issues that plague the Latino community are not the digital divide. It's the Latino Divide, and it must be fixed before we can meaningfully change the decision making that is almost always imposed on our community. The African American community has found its voice because it has united. They are at the decision-making table in ways that run circles around the Latino community, but the Hispanic community's issue is that it is divided, especially during the four years of President Trump's administration. It would take a once-in-a-century, moderate, coalition-building Latino leader to knit our communities together cohesively with a coherent story that helps us realize our fullest potential.

Manny's first company was Hispanic PR Wire, which he launched in 2008 and then sold in seven years for $5.5 million to his longtime competitor PR Newswire (now Cision). Following that transaction Manny become the founder of the Latino social media and marketing industry with the company Hispanicize, which he sold two years later. This established his reputation as a successful media mogul, but today he is infinitely prouder of his current career chapter. Now, Manny is the cofounder and senior partner in the next generation ventures of what both of those companies would have been today. Brilla Media is the successor to Hispanicize and Latinx Newswire and represents what he calls Hispanic PR Wire 3.0.

Even though it may be accurate to say he is a serial media entrepreneur, he would like to think of himself as a journalist for life, because he went into the media industry as a reporter to help save the world. Today, he is the proud cofounder and senior partner in various media and content distribution ventures, including Brilla Media, Latinx Newswire, Pop Culture Newswire, and RetroPop Media. All of these ventures are knit together by culture, storytelling, and guaranteed distribution, and that's what he is excited about the most.

With regards to diversity and inclusion, Manny's track record has always made him a bit of an outsider in the Hispanic community because he has been very public in saying we've variously been either anemic in the grip of Trump or have totally sold out to the Democratic Party that takes us for granted. Hollywood is also very *blasé* toward us because we don't demand a seat at the table.

Over the past two decades, Manny has had more than 25 business partners and at least 60 percent of them, including the main executives of his ventures, have been Latinas. This has been an organic choice: he doesn't feel a motive to be politically correct in hiring, but he will admit that he is proud to be a father of three little girls.

Latinos can succeed in media by harnessing the power of social media, and once they have established a consistent and large audience, determining how they will scale their audiences into businesses that are multifaceted, monetizable, and scalable. Maria Marin, for example, is a terrific model of someone who started as an influencer and today is rocketing into other ventures birthed from her sheer output of engaging, quality content. One of the biggest obstacles he sees from many Latinos in media and social media is that we don't know how to scale our platforms. He learned to do this with his previous two media ventures, but it was hard because the other problem many of us face is that we lack mentors in media who have actually succeeded. The fact that a Latino created and sold even one media company – let alone two – is extremely rare, and that rarity is disheartening. The other major challenge Latinos face is that media companies typically require capital to build, and many times we really don't know where to find this capital. Access to capital is a severe issue for Latino entrepreneurs, but especially for those in media.

Brilla Media provides brand marketers with innovative Latinx-branded entertainment, media, and experiential storytelling. The fact that Manny's company is Latino owned and operated is by itself unique – if not sad – because they are one of the only companies in the *entire* United States that offers proprietary premium video content distribution for brands via paid, owned, earned Media.

Brilla Media features five service pillars: Brilla Media (distribution), Brilla Live (festivals and livestreams), Brilla Creative (original storytelling), Brilla Social (influencer and social media amplification), and Brilla Purpose (social good).

To do what they do and say that they are authentically Latino-owned and operated should not be a headline and something they encourage brands that want to work with Latino-owned and operated companies to delve into with their competitors.

Maria Cardona
Principal at the Dewey Square Group
CNN Political Commentator

She believed she could, so she did.

– R.S. Grey

Maria Cardona was born in Bogotá, Colombia, and was around two and a half years old when her family arrived in the United States seeking better opportunities for her father to make a living and for them to have a brighter future. They settled in Florida and her father began work as an engineer with the Florida Telephone Company. Her father had the privilege of going to college in Colombia but her mother had only a high school education. So, Maria is the first woman in her family to graduate from college. Maria was very lucky to have parents who encouraged her from when she was a little girl and pushed her to go beyond any perceived limits.

One of Maria's favorite stories, told to her by her dad later in life, was how when he finally had the opportunity to be a decision-maker in his department at the Florida Telephone Company, he hired two women to be head engineers. That was a scandal! The men in her dad's department who were convinced they would get those jobs were furious! They demanded to know why her father had given these jobs, with prestige, power, and money, to *women*. How dare he choose women over the men who worked for him? When her father was confronted he simply said, "Because they were the best qualified." That was the extent of his explanations. With that simple but groundbreaking decision, her father changed the course of hiring at the company and opened a door that had been unavailable to women until that point.

Through these stories and others, Maria learned why her parents always encouraged her to live her life by assuming there were no limits. When an obstacle was put in front of her, she was taught to either knock it down or figure out a way around it. Maria was taught to assume she could do anything, not the other way around. Maria was taught that with hard work and the will to believe in herself, the sky was the limit.

Maria was extremely lucky to have had parents and mentors who believed she could succeed and who pushed her to do whatever she was interested in and who understood that her drive and her self-confidence would be her shield in a world that would try to stop a young Latina from achieving the heights of her dreams and aspirations. She wishes to tell her parents, "*Gracias, Papi, gracias, Mami!*"

Maria had the opportunity throughout her career to work on technology issues in the Latino community and understand all too well how this divide has kept way too many of our young children and young adults from achieving what could have been the heights they aspired to reach. It is ironic that a community that adapted faster to technology and at younger ages still has tremendous disadvantages in terms of access and having reliable technology, whether that means an internet connection at home or computers and tablets that can accommodate today's homework assignments that most children are getting from their teachers in the new normal of a virtual education.

Corporations can have transformational impact on the future of technology access to communities that have been historically left behind. Low-cost programs that provide broadband access either through a home internet connection or through smartphones can give families the connections they need to be able to access the critical services the internet provides. These days, healthcare, education, job-training services, college applications, job applications, and even keeping in touch with far-away family and friends can be done only with a strong enough broadband internet connection.

Companies in the technology sector can also have a positive impact by ensuring there is diversity within their ranks and make training programs for young engineers and/or internships available to those who aspire to work in these important tech and telecommunications fields.

Public policy solutions at the federal, state, and local level and academic institutions can be incredibly impactful as well. Public education needs to start prioritizing technology and a STEM (science, technology, engineering, and math) education at much younger ages and not just in high school. These curricula should be started in preschool so that all kids, from all backgrounds, and especially girls of color, understand that it is all within their reach and not something that is just available for the privileged few. We would all be better off if all our kids were to start accessing these valuable STEM subjects from the time they are able to look at a screen. This is the vital mission that Ad Astra Media is seeking to accomplish – Es Tiempo.

Maria is a principal at a nationally renowned public affairs firm where she leads the Latino Strategies and Multicultural Practices. She is also a CNN *en Español* political commentator. Maria has had the privilege of having a national platform – through her television commentary – but also through her columns and public speaking opportunities, to address issues of diversity, equity and inclusion. And she has always tried to put an emphasis on the importance of technology, telecommunications, and digital issues as areas where diversity needs to be front and center. Maria emphasizes that we have seen the data from high-tech firms in terms of what a dearth of diversity they have, and she calls it dismal and very discouraging. But that is where community activists, companies, and trailblazing leaders at these very same corporations can make transformational change – they just need to have the will to make it happen and use the data that exists to prove the problem is monumental and needs to change.

Data is imperative because it tells us where we are falling behind and where we need to do better. And we need to do better in all areas of the STEM fields. These jobs are by far better-paying jobs, and lead to more long-term stability for communities than other fields. We also need to push the leaders in these sectors to become allies of ours and work toward common goals. But what we must all understand is that we will not see the change we need until we see more people of color and Latinos and Latinas in the positions where these decisions are made – meaning on the boards of these corporations, as their CEOs, CFOs, COOs, and other C-suite offices. This is the ultimate goal and we cannot rest until we are there and our numbers equal what our population represents.

Diversity is front and center for all of us now, so now is the time when we need to make the boldest change. We know that diversity is beneficial for a company and that diversity and equity that truly represent a companies' consumers will give the biggest ROI to that very same company. It is not just the right thing to do but it is the best thing to do for stockholders and for the company's bottom line. A win-win, indeed!

Latinos can succeed in media by speaking out on behalf of our community and the issues that are important to us. When we tell our stories, our quintessential American stories, we *succeed*. When we ignore the negative voices in our heads telling us we don't matter, we *succeed*. And when we don't let other naysayers, or even doors being slammed in our faces, dissuade us from speaking out, speaking up, demanding a seat at the table, having the audacity to pull up a chair even when we are not invited, we *succeed*. There will always be obstacles, either real or perceived, either in our faces or in our minds. We can either choose to knock down these obstacles or figure out a way around them.

Maria has found that we need to come to the table prepared, having done our homework and our research. Knowing more than the person next to us. No excuses, because there may be no second chances. Especially for people who look like us or sound like us or have last names like us. That is the cold reality. Let's not let it be what defines us.

Pedro Guerrero
Chief Executive Officer
Cofounder of Alumni Society

> Between stimulus and response there is space. In that space is our power to choose our response. In our response lies our growth and freedom.
>
> — Viktor Frankl, *Man's Search for Meaning*

Pedro Guerrero grew up in Hayward, California. His mother and his family moved there from Zináparo, Michoacán, to reunite with his grandfather, who had landed a job at a local cannery. Back then, Hayward was a big canning town and the local canneries were some of its largest employers. His mother was the first to go to college in her family. She got her BA in education from California State University, Hayward.

His dad grew up on the East Coast and moved to California to attend Stanford, where he received his master's degree in education. One of his first teaching jobs was with the Hayward Unified School District. He met Pedro's mother when she walked into his classroom and introduced herself as his new teacher's assistant.

In many ways, he had a leg up on his classmates: both of his parents were educators and keenly aware of the challenges young Mexican American kids had growing up in a town like Hayward. The public high schools in Hayward were tough. There was a lot of gang activity and his circle of Latino friends was susceptible to being recruited by gangs. So, although they were public school educators, his parents explored other educational options for him. His mom had heard of a program called A Better Chance (ABC) and signed him up. ABC helps minority students attend preparatory schools, and through the help of the program, he received a scholarship to attend St. George's School, a private boarding school in Newport, Rhode Island.

St. George's opened up an entire universe of opportunities in his education and personal development. While there, he learned about liberal art colleges of which he was previously unfamiliar – like Bowdoin College in Brunswick, Maine, where he received his undergraduate degree.

Pedro has been thinking about the digital divide a lot these days, and it's real. There are many ways in which a lack of tech is hurting our progress, and there are many ways in which tech itself is holding us back. On the educational front, the threat of the digital divide is clear—and the COVID-19 pandemic exposed a massive weakness in our society.

Remote learning that's taken place over the past 12 to 18 months is going to have disastrous, generational consequences on not just the Latino community but also the African American community, immigrant communities, rural communities, and working families that do not have the luxury of working from home.

Many of these communities do not have the hardware – or even the internet service – to work remotely. Nor do they have the budget to pay for an increase in data usage on their monthly bills. Some immigrant communities don't have the opportunities to help students whose homework and lesson plans are in English. There's so much more at stake and at risk by keeping kids, especially Latino kids, out of school.

Then again, because we've long been divesting from public education, the chickens have come home to roost at the expense of students. We've been closing down schools, closing programs, not paying teachers enough, and allowing the student-teacher ratio to reach an unsustainable, and unhealthy, level.

We've essentially been defunding our future so much that we need smaller classrooms with state-of-the art HVAC, with state-of-the art technology, and with teachers who feel valued so that if, God forbid, we have a pandemic, *at least the kids have a safe place to congregate and learn.*

So, Pedro expresses how terribly concerned he is with the digital divide and his fear is this: 20 years from now when we wonder why the rates of incarceration in the Latino community have spiked or why there's an increase in Latinos dropping out of school, we're going to trace it back to the drought our community experienced in education, athletics, and socializing with peers. It will be like looking at the rings of a tree and finding exactly when the tree experienced drought. And for us, the experience will be severe.

To continue to evolve the Latino digital intelligence, Pedro believes we have to do three things in parallel. One, we need to build our own table. Pedro is naturally impatient and tired of waiting – so, time to build our own. Two, we need to continue to demand that companies include Latinos in their diversity efforts at all levels, from entry level to corporate director level. Three, we need to intentionally help other Latinos by opening doors, hiring them, procuring Latino vendors, and investing in Latino-owned companies.

We are intentional in selecting the executives we feature on the covers of our magazines, as well as those executives we profile in our newsletters and in our social media campaigns. We always promote the diversity of the executives we are privileged to profile. Doing so reduces the deficit of success stories from underrepresented communities.

So many of us are out there in plain sight, working hard. His team has an intentionality—each and every time they develop content—to promote their work with the lens of DEI.

Since he founded Guerrero in 2006, they have been focused on connecting with executives, getting to know them, and sharing their narratives across the brands they own. Their most well known of those brands is *Hispanic Executive*, which has provided us with the luxury to recognize and promote the depth of Latino leadership in our business community.

At a *Hispanic Executive* event in 2015, where we honored executives featured in our Top 10 Líderes issue, he met honoree, Ricardo Anzaldua, who at the time was the EVP and GC of Metlife. They both started talking about creating a new network for Latinos who shared similar academic experiences. That network would not only drive value to its members but also help a company like Metlife meet top Latino talent. The conversation set the groundwork for what would become the Alumni Society, which as of today is a network of over 4,800 Latinos who attended some of the top schools in the country.

The Alumni Society has been fortunate to partner with companies like Facebook, Goldman Sachs, TPG, Nike, and Sequoia Capital, each of which understands the value of making meaningful connections with Latinos for senior level positions.

They have also recently launched a retained search service, offering further proof that Guerrero has evolved into more than just a publisher—they sit at the center of content, professional networks, and executive search services with a focus on DEI.

Become teachers. Become school administrators. Run for office – be it with a school board or a city council. We need a hand in directing and crafting educational policy. Pedro is excited that with the confirmation of Miguel Cardona as secretary of education, we now have an educator and a Latino in a top job of an administration. We need to keep demanding that our stories are included in the historical narrative of American history and not just heard during Hispanic Heritage Month.

Pedro also recalls his familial experience and what he heard at the dinner table listening to his parents talk about work. Having parental involvement is critical for a student's success. A child's education doesn't stop at the school's doors. It's important that there is a line of communication and respect between the parents and the teachers. Language barriers and cultural gaps need to be crossed. Responsibility lies with the schools, so they need to have the emotional and cultural awareness to be able to connect with parents. This is another major component to the continued evolution of Latino digital intelligence.

Carlos Pérez
Creative Director
Art Origin

> An idea can turn to dust or magic, depending on the talent that rubs against it.
>
> — William Bernbach

Carlos Pérez was born in Mexico City, but grew up in El Chante, a small town outside Guadalajara. There, for a period of time, he was separated from his mother, who had come to the United States to work and send money back home. During her absence, his aunts served as his surrogate parents. "They had tremendous faith in me," he recalls. They would always tell him, "*Vas a hacer cosas grandes.*" That faith gave him the permission to dream and the confidence to know that what he dreamed could be a reality.

In 1972, Carlos was accepted into the Art and Design Program at San José State University under the EOP Program and received a grant in order to attend higher education. Had it not been for the EOP program he would not have been able to get a university education.

But let's talk about the time he drew the Apple logo. Like any self-respecting technophile, Carlos eschews any mention of honors or awards when asked of his achievements and goes straight to the tools of his trade. He can recap every detail associated with his past projects with photographic clarity. For example, he can tell you the weight of the pencil, the opacity of the tissue, and the precise angle of every stroke he used to create the first sketches of the Apple logo.

But even these aspects of his work come to him as an afterthought. It's when he talks about his artistic origins that his voice catches and he discusses some of his most vivid memories – memories that have surprisingly little to do with Silicon Valley and the burgeoning technological revolution that would set the stage for his work as a graphic artist. This transformative time would serve as a precursor to another.

The design industry was one of the first to be reinvented by the digital age. Like any transition, this brought the end of an old state, complete with a set of tools and techniques that had remained relatively constant until then. But unlike previous transitions, the industry's new state wasn't just new, it was ever-changing. The space it came to inhabit is normal now but was alien at the time — a world of constant updates and mandatory upgrades, where planned obsolescence is the only thing anyone can predict.

As a designer on the first marketing communications team to manage the Apple account, Carlos's work gestured toward the change about to come. In his portfolio are numerous collateral design and production assets used to help launch the Apple II. Anyone who used the Apple II could never forget it. With its 1-megahertz processor and 4-kilobyte memory, it teleported middle schoolers everywhere. Who can forget the iconic game "The Oregon Trail"? It turned fourth-period classrooms into small-game hunting preserves. It was 11 pounds of beige bliss. It was also the first time a lot of kids — especially those of working-class backgrounds — ever explored the world of computing.

In 1977, Carlos Pérez and Rob Janoff were colleagues at Regis McKenna. Rob designed the Apple mark, while Carlos created its initial rendering and master artwork. Carlos also rendered the typographical solutions that would accompany the Apple logo brand, designed and art-directed the first Apple newsletter, and created the masthead for and code-signed the first Apple magazine. He inked all of this by hand, relying on his mastery of drafting and illustration techniques, because the hardware and applications now ubiquitous in the realm of graphic design simply did not yet exist.

Carlos recalls this era with a kind of excitement that's difficult to put into words. It's in his eyes when he talks about the long-haired, torn-jeaned Steve Jobs walking in to talk shop, like it was no big deal. It's there when he reflects on the talent that helped inspire him, specifically, the design team consisting of Rob Janoff, James Ferris, Lee Beggs, Mauricio Arias, and others who, he says, "paved the way for the most recognizable mark on the planet."

It is appropriate that at a time when most people were still groping in the dark for their on switches and screaming insults at their dot matrix printers, Carlos was doing some of the best design of his life. Upheavals were nothing new to him. Like other professional Latinos, he had transitioned between worlds before.

As a boy, his creative aspirations were so apparent that his aunts arranged for him to apprentice with a local artist. By 1972, he was in the United States, studying art and design at

San José State University. Two years later he was awarded an apprenticeship by the Western Arts Director's Club, an honor reserved for only the top three graduates. This apprenticeship began another, at the prestigious advertising firm of Regis McKenna. He struck out on his own in 1980 with Carlos Pérez Design, Inc., now known as ArtOrigin. Here he has done work for both IBM and Hewlett Packard, leading design teams that helped launch product systems and develop typographical character systems. Today Carlos is working on publishing a book and on developing his own line of creative products based on his Latino/Chicano cultural heritage.

One of his ongoing commissions is with the Cinequest Film Festival. Pérez is the designer of the Festival's Maverick Spirit Award, which he has personally presented to Kevin Spacy, James Olmos, Sir Ben Kingsley, Lupe Ontiveros, Diablo Cody, William H. Macy, Spike Lee, Lalo Schifrin, Danny Glover, and Benjamin Bratt.

When asked about the things that drive him most today, Carlos comes back to family and community. His extended family includes a writer, photographer, nurse, make-up artist, communications major, three grandchildren, and his wife and business partner, Analisa, all of whom live and work in San José. A product of the 1960s Chicano Student Movement, Carlos considers community-building through the arts as central to his life as a creative professional and works consistently with South Bay nonprofits and arts organizations to connect art to the communities it serves. He hopes this will help "foster a cultural climate where creative thinkers are treated as professionals with equal credentials and not as third-class citizens." In such partnerships, he sees the importance of technology and abstract ideas, but he emphasizes the role of individual creativity "I'm reminded of a quote from advertising guru Bill Bernbach," he says. "An idea can turn to dust or magic depending on the talent that rubs against it."

We need to develop and support critical thinking skills in young people's lives . . . "I believe that STEM is not enough, we need to think STEAM," says Carlos, which is at the core of Ad Astra Media. We must make community-building through the arts as central to life as creative professionals.

Simón Silva
Artist and Motivational Speaker

> Our greatest asset is not going to be found in our education, position or possessions, it is going to be found in our wonderful individuality.
>
> — Simón Silva

Simón Silva was born in Mexicali, Mexico, in 1961 and came to the United States when he was just over one year old. He is one of 11 children, and he is still the only first-generation college graduate from his family. The obstacles he faced to get to college and succeed were many, starting with the fact that he was dirt poor. Growing up, his greatest obstacle was his parents' misunderstanding about what education is and what it is for. Both of his parents believed education was a complete waste of time, probably because of their limited education, which ended after the third grade. There never was any support for his education from his parents and his overall family. He also grew up in a town and went to a school that still viewed Latino students as being limited in abilities and academic success. He also felt that not knowing what to expect from the educational process was limiting him, especially in choosing a career, so he felt that art was going to provide him with the greatest degree of success.

There are still great numbers of families that have limited or no access to the internet or the ability to buy adequate computer equipment. Simón also continues to encounter individuals in the corporate and educational world who have limited knowledge about the role that the arts can play in creating life-long, creative individuals. Most educators believe the arts are simply a way to get students to follow directions and improve on their hand and eye coordination. There is also a tendency for most people to believe that the arts in general are irrelevant to a person's overall educational experience – most school districts misuse the arts and disrespect the arts. They believe that most children don't know how to draw and thus the disrespect of the arts continues to negatively affect the creativity and individuality of most students.

Throughout history we have put too much importance on technology; we believed that typewriters were going to make us better communicators, the internet was going to make us smarter, and yet these things have not done that at all. Technology and the digital age have given us tools, but information is just information until the individual is able to process and apply that information. It is critical for that individual to have the ability to apply their knowledge to a creative new concept or to solve problems. He believes that all of us at one point had about 90 percent of the so-called "twenty-first-century skills," and most of that was negatively affected by a lack of knowledge by parents and the education system. We can promote equity and inclusion by simply becoming aware of how the arts can continue to nurture and develop everyone's individuality and creativity, regardless of race, gender, or social class. Until we create a level playing field, things will not change for the masses.

The arts are not necessarily only to create great pieces of art – when taught correctly/effectively they can become an extension of our life-long learning and create secure, creative minds. So first we need to redefine success and make sure that our perception of success includes more than just financial wealth; it should include individuality, social consciousness, political involvement, and a need to change things for future generations. We need to have artists who are willing to take risks, have something to say, and have something they would like to explore. Creating pretty images or reiterating old images are not going to change the views of anyone. We need to bring respect for the arts and help create a sense of respect and value for those who practice the arts. Visit www.simonsilva.com.

7

Leverage
Venture Capital and Entrepreneurship

—

Alicia Castillo-Holley
Founder
Wealthing VC Club
I'm not the victim of my circumstances but the master
of my choices.

— Alicia Castillo-Holley

ALICIA CASTILLO-HOLLEY LIVED FOR THE first five years of her life in
Acarigua, and then grew up in El Limon, Venezuela; although
she was born in Caracas, she never lived there. Her father
finished college and put a lot of emphasis on the importance
of education. Alicia is the first one in her family to have two
masters and a PhD, and she was the valedictorian of her
undergraduate class.

Alicia also received her MBA and has a family. She believes
all things are possible through hard work. So, she recalls that

she never saw any challenges or obstacles in her path; she was always focused.

Alicia had her children young, and got divorced young. At the age of 26, she had two kids and was a single mother. She didn't think it would be any other way, so she became busy making a magic life for them. Alicia remembers not sleeping much, making her kids part of her dream, and taking them to libraries and schools to make them part of her success.

It is natural to expect that Latinos feel uncomfortable and uneasy when dealing with investors and advisors who do not share our intuitive knowledge about how to do businesses and how to socialize in general. A study made by an anthropologist in Africa years ago showed that Latinos were more likely to trust someone from their close network than a consultant. It is no different from any other human group. We are self-organizing through familiar tribal knowledge and patterns. Anyone raised in a group that does not talk about high-impact high-growth companies is at a natural disadvantage, because he or she does not have the intuitive knowledge and feels out of place.

The third factor is the invisible discount of Latinas' capacity to execute. Both as a founder and as an investor, Alicia experienced this discounting factor. It took her longer to get into meetings with the appropriate person, to hire the most talented person, and to get appropriate terms of engagement for almost any business transaction. This has a cost and, in the case of women in general, has been called the pink tax. Services and products offered by Latinas have a lower perceived value, and service providers usually charge more. As a Latina investor, her capacity to execute is often doubted as well. Many people didn't think Alicia could finish an MBA as a single mother; she sometimes didn't know if she would have enough money for food, and she and her children slept on the floor. When people learned more about her, they graciously went out of their way to give the family coats or beds (her amazing landlord came to fix something and saw that they didn't have beds), and invited them for meals. Alicia thinks that keeping her challenges to herself helped them a lot.

In her view, success is a choice; we choose to be successful – however we define it – and we act upon that.

Latinos have funds; we just don't trust each other, and truth does not have the same meaning for everyone – not just for Latinos.

We need to be accountable for our sense of decency and transparency, for our need to ask for support. We also need to be better at managing data, and not just intuition, and for hiring and delegating to people who are smarter than us.

Last, Latinos need to have healthy boundaries with their relatives and communities. It is an uphill battle to be the ATM machine for the community. Poor people have the same issue. Wealthier people don't have these issues because there is more wealth. When you have a whole town or block that does not understand how difficult it has been for you or how to respect your individual wealth, then you create a barrier. The same happens with Africans or poor whites. We have to solve those problems too.

In summary, Alicia does not have control over the VC sector but she does have control over her actions, and that is what she focuses on. There are plenty of people who believed in her despite where she came from and had a significant impact on her accomplishments.

Alicia is an active angel investor and is the founder of the Wealthing VC Club, where members coinvest in post-seed deals and give accredited investors the opportunity to learn how to spot high-quality deals from sophisticated investors. Her goal is that by doing that, investors who could become angels learn to do so more professionally, and, given the shorter times to exit, could have returns earlier to keep lifting the bar in their communities.

It is too complicated and impractical to give inexperienced founders inexperienced investors. Alicia is giving inexperienced investors the opportunity to interact with experienced founders, to analyze deals with experienced investors, and make their own investment decisions.

Alicia is one of the many Latinos/Latinx who are successful. If we learn how to be authentic (unfortunately, there are many fake investors), humble, and trustworthy, our chances of building a healthy ecosystem increase.

Alicia doesn't believe in the word "help." Alicia supports people who cannot support themselves. The appropriate term is *support* or *champion*. We could start right away by highlighting the many successful Latinos in the industry.

Beatriz Acevedo
CEO and Cofounder
Suma Wealth

Never feel less or intimidated for being the "only one" that looks like you in a room full of "sameness"; being different is your superpower! Lean hard into it and be proud of being different, being unique, and having diverse points of view. This is what makes you incredibly valuable.

– Beatriz Acevedo

Beatriz Avecedo is a proud border girl. She was born in Tijuana, Mexico, because her father wanted her to be president of Mexico one day. He rushed Beatriz's mother across the border from San Diego in time for the birth. This makes Beatriz an immigrant even though her family resided in the United States. Having one foot in Mexico and another one in the United States while growing up shaped her into who she is today: a hybrid of the best of both worlds with a mash-up culture of which she is very proud.

Both of her parents were college educated (the first in their families to go to college), and Beatriz is actually the least formally college educated in her family. Her mom has a PhD in psychology and her brother a master's in international law. She was not very excited to go to college as she was already deeply involved in her work as a journalist (or at least she fancied herself as one!) and she loved her work. Beatriz began working in radio and later in television from when she was eight years old, so she was looking forward to graduating from high school to be able to work full time. But her mom did not let her do that; it was not cool back then to be a college dropout, as is it today in Silicon Valley when bright teenagers become tech entrepreneurs. To this day her mom asks Beatriz when she is going to enroll in a master's degree program. "Never say never," Beatriz replies, but it is not in her immediate plans. She believes having an education is critical but there are many roads to success and for some professions – like hers – where it's all about the hustle. Your life experiences are as critical as college.

The American economy will depend on the success of Latinos as well as other groups. It's a numbers game and we can't have a cohort this large with so many disparities and inequalities, including access to the internet. We see kids in our community having to do homework on their phones because of poor or no access to the internet at home, and this is heartbreaking. These are the young men and women who will be responsible for paying Social Security taxes on behalf of *all* eligible Americans. We need to empower them with the tools they need to succeed so that all Americans can succeed. This is the message we need to drill into everyone's heads. It's not a Latino problem, it's an American problem, and we need to fix it fast. In Los Angeles she is very proud to support several organization in the tech and VC sectors, as well as in philanthropy. Beatriz is actively involved in helping to close the digital divide, as she hopes Latinos in Los Angeles can be a model for others in the state and the country as well.

Beatriz is an entrepreneur and a philanthropist. She always does business within the Latino community. She hires from the Latino community and her office is open on a daily basis. She is very aware that she is an outlier when it comes to her ability to raise capital, sit on prominent boards, and be at the tables where decisions are being made. She never forgets the responsibility she has to bring others along because of this privilege. There is room for everyone. We are so underrepresented in every single sector, not just in venture capital but also in media. This is critical to how others and how we perceive ourselves and what it is possible to achieve. Beatriz is very active in trying to change this, particularly in venture capital.

She has been cochairing a board that works hard to address this. PledgeLA (www.pledgela.org) is led by the Annenberg Foundation and the mayor of Los Angeles, Eric Garcetti. Beatriz mentions they have over 200 tech and VCs in the city actively working to make our tech ecosystem more inclusive and representative of what Los Angeles looks like. Latinos are almost half of this city, and when they started these efforts a couple of years back, Latinos only got 2 percent of the funding. Now we are at 6 percent, but there is still a lot of work ahead of us. She is part of the progress we have made, thanks to the commitment of our Angelino tech and venture capital community.

Beatriz emphasizes that we need more people at the top who are like us, leading both funds and tech companies. That is really the solution. But while we are getting there, we need the help of white male allies who are still the decision-makers determining who gets funded. We need them to see the opportunity in the Latino community.

For Beatriz, it's a business decision that is smart, not a charity. Latinos are the cohort to bet on for so many reasons. They are so much younger than any other cohort; they are entering the workforce at an accelerated rate, replacing boomers; they are driving GDP growth; they are more than ever enrolled in college; and the list goes on and on. So, if you want to future-proof your business and succeed in the future, this will not happen without Latinos on your side. It's pure math.

We need to support our community and our entrepreneurs *now*, because the American economy is dependent on their success, particularly the success of the women. Latinas are launching more companies than any other cohort but are also the ones who receive the least amount of capital to grow their businesses. Inside the workforce, Latinas are still the female group that has the largest pay gap disparity – losing an average of over a million dollars *each* in their productive careers. The Latino community is hard working and resilient. Beatriz has no doubt they will succeed, but why not help accelerate their success?

Erika Lucas
Cofounder
StitchCrew

Perfection and growth don't coexist.

— Erika Lucas

Erika Lucas was born and raised in Mexico. Although she attended college, she didn't graduate. The main obstacles she experienced were financial, of course. She started working at an early age to be able to provide for herself; managing work and college hours was hard for her, but she did it.

Erika is an experiential learner. This caused her to feel very out of place while completing her thesis, as opposed to working and getting her hands dirty.

Erika first migrated to Oklahoma when she was 13 years old, with her then single mother and younger sister. Erika didn't know a lick of English, so not only did she have to adapt to cultural changes, but she also had to learn the language. After a couple of years, she went back to Mexico to live with her *abuelitos*. That's where she started her career helping multinational companies offshore their operations to Mexico. Later in life, while visiting her mom in Oklahoma, she met her husband, and the rest is history.

In Oklahoma, she spent six years working as the global director for the Oklahoma Department of Commerce where she helped existing businesses expand into international markets and recruited foreign direct investment (FDI) into the state. One of the industries they heavily recruited was aerospace and defense (A&D), so after her public service, she went to work as partner of a private equity firm that invested exclusively in A&D in the United States and Europe. That's when Erika came across the ridiculous funding gap that exists for women and entrepreneurs of color and realized she was not going to be able to do much to change that by working with later-stage investments. That's when she launched StitchCrew and partnered with Oklahoma City Thunder to run an accelerator program.

Her experience working with an NBA team and the franchise has been outstanding. They feel that their mission is very much aligned to create a more inclusive and equitable economy in their region. Sports teams are one of the greatest motivators of our time. They inspire commitment, dedication, and risk taking. Sports teams also teach us a thing or two about an individual's ability to push limits and manage success and failure as a learning step to becoming great. Moreover, sports teams tend to be inclusive, diverse, and unscripted. These cultural characteristics are critical traits of successful entrepreneurs and thriving start-up communities.

We need to change the face of who is writing the checks. With less than 3 percent of Black and Brown venture capitalists, LPs, and angel investors, we can easily correlate the disproportionate amount invested in entrepreneurs of color. We also need to understand and help entrepreneurs who need support outside of venture capital. Different types of businesses require different types of capital. While venture capital is amazing, it is not always the right option for certain business models and growth trajectories. If we help Latinx entrepreneurs gain better understanding of the type of capital they need based on their growth, they are more likely to secure it. Beyond capital, LOBs also need convenient and culturally competent business training to build the business acumen needed to increase revenue and reach scale. Offering support and guidance on how to grow and compound revenue, manage human and capital resources, and how to structure a business for maximum return is crucial to help them reach scale.

Erika is the cofounder of StitchCrew, an organization focused on building a more equitable economy through entrepreneurship. She is also the founder of VEST, a curated network of women working together to expedite the pipeline of more women in positions of power and influence. She talks about the funding gap and bias that exist for women and people of color in her TED Talk, America's Trillion Dollar Blindspot. Diversity is not something we do, it is who we are and why we exist.

Latino entrepreneurs are starting new companies at more than twice the rate of all other groups combined. Yet, only 3 percent of those Latino owned businesses reach scale ($1 million or more in annual revenue on a sustained basis).

Get to the point where you are not just doing due diligence and taking notes for partners but writing checks! Build your network, leverage relationships, and don't preach to the status quo. The status quo benefits from keeping things the way they are, so don't waste your time preaching to them; instead, find allies.

Alberto Yepez
Cofounder and Managing Director
ForgePoint Capital

The harder I work, the luckier I get.

– Alberto Yepez

Alberto grew up in Tacna, the southernmost city of Peru, close to the border with Chile and in the middle of the Atacama Desert. Alberto is a third-generation college graduate. His father and grandfather were lawyers who served as judges in the cities of Cuzco and Tacna (Perú).

Alberto studied Electronic Engineering at the Universidad Nacional de Ingenieria in Lima (1 of 33 universities in the country). It was a very competitive admission process: 40,000 applicants, 2,000 spots, and the first 200 selected electronic engineering as a major. At that time, the Jesuit Missionaries from California had established the Cristo Rey School in Tacna, and awarded Alberto a Presidential Scholarship to study at the University of San Francisco (USF).

He completed his Bachelor of Science (BS) degree at USF with a triple major: electronic physics, computer science, and computer engineering. In 1986, he was recruited by Apple as a network design engineer. He spent 10 years at Apple working on a variety of positions of increased responsibility.

After 10 years, he left Apple and bootstrapped his first start-up with his wife. They almost took the company public after raising four rounds of venture capital. In 2000, the company was acquired for $1 billion.

The digital divide in the Latino and Latinx community is real, due to the lack of education and role models that encourage our community to pursue careers in STEM. We need to support individuals participating in the innovation economy, for example Sand Hill Road and Venture Capital Community, as well as entrepreneurs and organizations that foster science education programs and offer internships to prepare the next generation of Latino and Latinx technology leaders.

Alberto mentions how we can change the narrative by getting involved and lead by example, recruiting, mentoring, and sponsoring emerging leaders in our communities to pursue careers in science and help them land internships to prepare them to join the work force. We should sponsor internships and scholarships when possible.

We need to create new role models at every level, as well as act as role models to show the next generation that it is possible to succeed by pursuing higher education and hard work.

Alberto started his career as a venture capitalist, but he has worked with many large corporations over the course of his career, including Apple and Oracle. He has held various positions, including CEO of EnCommerce, Entrust, and Thor Technologies. He began his venture capital career at Trident Capital in 2010. He later cofounded ForgePoint Capital, which is the largest VC cybersecurity firm, with approximately $750 million in assets under management.

Alberto has witnessed firsthand the lack of diversity within the VC world. He at times has been the lone diverse representation on some boards. Because of this, he is passionate about diversity, equity, and inclusion. He is an active promoter of attaining 50/50 gender and minority representation on VC boards. And he is an active participant in several groups seeking to do the same, including the International Consortium of Minority Cybersecurity Professionals (ICMCP) and Women in Cybersecurity.

This is why ForgePoint Capital is a founding signatory for impact investing in the United Nations Principles for Responsible Investments and the ILPA Diversity in Action Initiative. They published the FPC ESG Handbook and encourage all the portfolio companies at the board level to adopt these principles and invest in diversity and inclusion and ESG initiatives.

In order for Latinos/Latinx to be successful in venture capital, they should obtain meaningful operational experiences to help entrepreneurs build successful companies. The most successful venture capitalist has prior experience leading functional areas in large corporations or founding his or her own start-ups.

It is very hard to break into the VC community without operational or investment experience. There are no short-cuts. Cybersecurity is at the heart of our daily lives and the digital transformation of businesses. They should pursue educational programs, internship programs, or apprentice-ship programs to learn the industry.

There is a huge opportunity for Latinos to excel with the VC community. Currently, there is a large shortage of skilled leaders in this industry. There are close to 1 million job openings for qualified candidates. This is an opportunity that the Latino community must seize. Go out. Get internships. Seek out mentors and sponsors. Obtain certifications and join community organizations, such as HITEC, ICMCP, and Es Tiempo.

Marcelo De Santis
Executive Advisor, Digital Transformation, Thought Works
President and Board Member, Angeles Investors

Whether you think you can, or you think you can't – you're right.

– Henry Ford

Marcelo De Santis was born in Buenos Aires, Argentina. His family has a strong Italian background. Both his grandfather and grandmother immigrated to Argentina after the war as a way to rebuild their lives after losing almost everything they had. His father was the first of their three sons to be born in Argentina. His father met his mother when she was 25, and they were married after a few years. They named their son Marcelo – Spanish for Marcello, the Italian version of his name. That did not discourage his grandmother and grandfather from calling him Marcello.

He went to Catholic school – Don Bosco – for both his primary and secondary school. During those years, he had the opportunity to learn the importance of working for those in need, such as joining initiatives to get kids back to school and support building programs to provide food and shelter to those that lack a home

Marcelo got into a university – University Argentina de la Empresa – right after secondary school to study Computer Science. He graduated in five years. As soon as he started, his father bought him a PC XT – a luxury in those times – and he started to build software in the very early stages of his career. Shortly, he became an entrepreneur (without knowing it!) by building a company that produced software for law firms. He sold the company at the age of 21. He remembers he used the proceedings to buy new appliances for his mother and to attend UC Berkeley to study English and business administration. That was his first trip to the United States and was going to change his life. After that he came back to Argentina and after two years he returned to the United States to work for Kraft Foods in New York City. That was the beginning of a corporate career that took him to San Francisco, Chicago, Singapore, China, and Italy, playing different executive roles as chief information officer and chief digital officer of companies like Kraft Foods, Mondelez, and Pirelli.

Today, he shares his time between consulting with companies on digital transformation as part of ThoughtWorks, supporting Latinx entrepreneurs with Angeles Investors (an angel group dedicated to help Latinx founders to grow their businesses), and growing the impact of Hispanic executives in technology as an executive coach and board member of HITEC.

Life is too short to spend a day without doing something for others. On one side, we (Latinx) are a large part of the U.S. population and a pretty young demographic that adapts technology and digital habits at a fast pace.

On the other side, due to the pandemic, many school districts that provided remote-only learning during the pandemic have – unintentionally – created a disadvantage for millions of children. This is because approximately 16.9 million children under the age of 18 lack high-speed home internet. One in three Black, Latino, and American Indian households lack internet access, making children in those homes more likely than their white peers to be disconnected from the ability to attend school and learn online.

There is an opportunity for corporations, our government, and nongovernment organizations to collaborate together to close this gap, which is not only putting a mortgage on the education of many children in this country but is also perpetuating inequalities that already divide countries and communities. Children and young people from the poorest households are falling even further behind their peers and are left with very little opportunity to ever catch up, making the digital divide even deeper. For us in the Latinx community, this is a higher calling to fight for closing the digital divide for "all children," to lead the change that we want for us, to the benefit of everyone.

Marcelo is proud of UNICEF and what they are doing in this area. In 2019, UNICEF and the International Telecommunications Union, a United Nations agency, launched Giga, a global initiative to connect every school in the world to the internet and every student to information, opportunity, and choice by 2030. Keep in mind that half of humanity still does not have access to the internet. It's a long road, but a good start has been made.

Marcelo has spent the past 25 years as a technology executive in different Fortune 500 companies, driving business transformation and building operating models where technology is at the core. Some call this digital transformation, and he wonders jokingly if anyone is driving any analog transformation these days. As Marcelo worked with startups in the corporate world, he noticed that the amount of Latinx founders was almost nonexistent. This observation made him curious, and after doing some research he found statistics showing that only 2 percent of the VC funding went to minority investors, and less than that for Latinx founders. He asked, what can we do to change this? This was the inspiration to build Angeles Investors, an angel group primarily dedicated to find, fund, and grow the most promising Latinx ventures.

Today, they have about 70 *angeles* who have deployed around $3 million in capital across almost 10 start-ups led by Latinx founders, and they report that almost 50 percent of the start-ups that they found are led by Latinas, which makes Marcelo extremely proud. They also are proud of not only helping the founders with capital for their start-ups but also providing the opportunity to Latinx individuals who are interested in investing in early-stage start-ups to learn together with the Angeles Investors. Finally, if you take into consideration that this was achieved in only 14 months and in the middle of the pandemic, Marcelo believes the results are amazingly incredible.

Marcelo also gives a big thank-you to Frank Carbajal for the support he has given to Angeles Investors. Marcelo still remembers that when he shared the idea of Angeles Investors on a Zoom call, it took only a few minutes for Frank to jump in.

Marcelo states that we need to unite ourselves. We need to relentlessly help each other and lead the change. While the statistics of 2 percent of VC funding going to minorities is something that bothers him, he does not want us in the Latinx community to victimize ourselves. We need to take control of the situation, thus – as Frank would say – "it is time," *es tiempo*, to own the problem, reframe it as an opportunity, leave our egos behind, and organize ourselves to provide capital to the great businesses that are being created and led by amazing Latinas and Latinos across this country.

This does not mean to do "charity" and invest in businesses that are not up to the challenge. This means committing to grow those businesses that are good and have potential and actively help the founders of those that have less potential to reinvent themselves and look for different opportunities. We need to lead this change anchored in the potential of our Latinx entrepreneur, with candid feedback and a helping hand. For instance, in Angeles they have seen around 150 start-ups and selected only around 20 for their pitch nights.

One of the challenges that Latinxs face in regards to access funding is the lack of awareness of the different options to obtain capital for their business. While they take a lot of pride in being a self-funded business, that is not a recipe to scale with agility as things improve. That combined with what Marcelo mentioned regarding the lack of VC funding going to minorities compounds the challenges for our Latinx community. But they can change that, and we will, together.

Angeles Investors – they call it "Angeles" – is an angel group primarily dedicated to find, fund, and grow the most promising Latinx ventures. They focus on start-ups that have a founder, board member, or main investor who is Hispanic or Latinx, at the seed stage or series A stage, preferably with a lead investor. They prioritize ventures in which technology is at the core of the business model.

As with any other angel group, you need to be an accredited investor to join Angeles – as defined by the SEC – pay an annual membership fee, and commit to a minimum annual investment amount (it's a soft commitment). From there you have access to their curated deal flow, exclusive, closed-doors pitch nights, and access to plenty of educational material and webinars on angel investment along with meeting great

Latinx investors, founders, and executives that make our community unique, interesting, and highly engaged.

Marcelo strongly believes that your mindset is your most important "muscle." Believing in yourself and having the perseverance to go through the highs and lows that life will – inevitably – throw your way is a mind game. A few years ago, he almost lost his life while climbing Everest. He remembers that at one point his lungs were so compromised that his body started to shut down. He sat down and felt cold and peaceful. He could not think about getting up on his feet, and he had no energy left. Fortunately, his climbing partner, Tindu, an amazing sherpa from Nepal and an even more amazing human being, showed him a picture of his wife that he used to carry in his backpack. When he looked at the picture, his energy suddenly came back and he got on his feet to then negotiate the infamous Khumbu icefall until – after a long, painful descent – he arrived at the medical tent at base camp to then be evacuated to Kathmandu. Was it a miracle? Marcelo does not know. But he does believe that our mind can move mountains, and that day his mind moved the mountain – gently – out of his way.

Sergio Monsalve
Founding Partner at Roble Ventures

Sergio Monsalve arrived in the United States from Mexico at the age of 13. He and his family moved to Bonita, California, with Spanish as his only language at the time. Sergio was a driven kid, understanding that in the United States, education is the equalizer.

Sergio got a Bachelor of Science degree in management science and engineering from Stanford University, and a masters of business administration from Harvard. Sergio was a venture partner at Norwest Venture Partners in Palo Alto, where he was a successful founder/entrepreneur, technology product manager, and operator at companies including eBay, PayPal, and various other start-ups.

He is actively involved as an investor and/or board member in several relevant ed-tech and "future of work" companies, including Udemy, the leading global online lifelong learning and teaching marketplace with over 19 million students, 20,000 instructors, and 96 million course enrollments; Kahoot, a K–12 learning application with over 50 million active users in more than 180 countries; and Adaptive Insights, a financial planning software solution with over 3,500 clients focused on the future of work. Sergio has seen firsthand the disparities of the educational gap between both sides of the freeway in the Silicon Valley on Route 101 from east to west.

Sergio has perceived that life in Silicon Valley is comprised of two worlds. As you're driving up the Peninsula on Route 101, you can see the east side of the freeway – predominantly Latino, Spanish-speaking families, with very little, slow broadband access and Wi-Fi – and on the west side of the freeway you can see some of the most expensive homes in the world in Atherton, Menlo Park, and Los Altos Hills, with access to the whole world.

Sergio has been inspired to help elevate the Latinx community. He has also been an active entrepreneurship mentor at Stanford's School of Engineering for over five years and is also a repeat member of the Stanford Class of 1993 Reunion

Committee. He also serves on the Board of Trustees at Harvey Mudd College, a leading undergraduate College for computer science, engineering, and science.

Sergio believes in fostering and helping develop new ideas at his alma mater, Stanford. Sergio believes we can make a big impact.

He has three teenage children and lives near campus. He was drawn to the position as an entrepreneur, a Stanford alumnus, and a parent. He believes that injecting the latest and greatest technologies into the educational world can yield great social impact and benefit many more people in the world in need of education.

He also believes that the future of work is transforming quickly, and that education and entrepreneurship can play a big role in helping our future workforce. Ultimately, he is excited about helping spur innovation around lifelong learning.

Sergio has been an investor, venture-funded entrepreneur, and operator of various global tech businesses in Silicon Valley. He is grateful to have been able to help three companies become multibillion-dollar unicorns.

He started his venture career as a partner at Norwest Venture Partners for 12 years. He invested early in Kahoot! ($6 billion), Udemy ($3.3 billion), and Adaptive Insights (sold to Workday for $1.6 billion), where he was on the board of directors for over six years. He is very excited about investing in technologies that help humans get ahead.

Sergio also cofounded Stanford's Entrepreneur-in-Residence Program at the Graduate School of Education, and he has been a lecturer at Stanford University. He coaches and mentors students on "Entrepreneurship and Innovation in Education Technology."

Sergio also has held various entrepreneurship and leadership roles in high-growth technology companies like eBay, PayPal, Portal Software (IPO during tenure), as well as various venture-backed start-ups he helped get off the ground as a founder or founding executive. Sergio is also on the board of trustees at Harvey Mudd College where he cochairs the entrepreneurial initiatives committee. He received a Bachelor of Science degree in Management Science and Engineering from Stanford University, and a Masters of Business Administration from Harvard.

Mario Ruiz
Investor
PayPal Ventures

> The genius of capitalism lies in its ability to make self-interest serve the wider interest.
>
> – Bill Gates

Mario Ruiz grew up in the Co-Op City section of the Bronx, New York, with his mother from Guatemala who came to this country as an undocumented immigrant and his father who came to New York as an adolescent from Puerto Rico. As a first-generation citizen and the first generation of his family to attend college, there were four key challenges that he faced to get to college and succeed:

1. **Access to information:** As a first-generation student in this country, he realized once he started working in corporate America that he did not have the requisite "play-

book" that his peers did (most of whom were from more privileged backgrounds and who had attended prestigious universities). He had no idea how to position himself in the college application process and did not have access to information on programs and resources that could help him to improve the core components of his college application, including his essay and test scores. Compared to his non-first-generation peers, he was at a disadvantage because his parents did not attend college and did not have learning or advice to impart.

2. **Quality of education:** Growing up in a low-income community in the Bronx, he was a high-achieving student in his public school, but when he began his career at a white-shoe investment bank, alongside peers who had attended private schools or public schools in well-funded areas, he noticed differences in the quality of education he had received.

3. **Challenges with self-confidence:** Mario grew up in a household where self-confidence was not encouraged and one where he was taught that "putting his head down, being humble, and doing good work" was the recipe for success. Due to that mental framework, he dealt with serious bouts of imposter syndrome when he began college and was around peers who were very confident in themselves and their abilities.

4. **Financial challenges:** While money does not solve all issues, growing up in a low-income household with financial challenges prohibited him from accessing resources to improve his college admissions story (e.g., music, the arts, sports) and precluded him from attending certain universities because cost was an issue.

In the 1990s, although computers started to become more widely adopted, he did not have access to a personal computer until much later in life (circa 2000). Instead, he had to rely on using a typewriter to type his homework assignments or stay at school after hours to access one of the two computers in his high school that served 840 students. In recent times, this digital divide has been exacerbated with the COVID-19 pandemic, where students are required to have access to reliable computers and internet to attend virtual classes. He believes this divide in access will continue to have compounding impacts in the future on those who aspire to matriculate into computer science and technology programs.

To change this narrative, we need more Latinos who are entering the industry through technology roles. He believes this will have a three-part impact: (1) more Latinos will become senior leaders within established technology giants and have influence in decision making, (2) more Latinos will decide to start their own companies and create generational wealth through large exits, and (3) we will see a shift of Latino engineers moving into senior-level roles at venture capital firms after years of success in product and engineering roles.

He is currently a principal at PayPal Ventures, the corporate venture capital (CVC) arm of PayPal, where he is responsible for investing in early and growth-stage fintech and commerce start-ups. Along with his direct investments, Mario helped spearhead PayPal's $530 million Economic Opportunity Fund commitment to invest in Black and other under-represented communities. As part of the commitment, he led their $100 million strategy in investing in emerging Black and Latinx fund managers.

Along with their fund investments, their ventures commitment also includes: (1) a three-month graduate fellowship for aspiring Black or Latinx venture capitalists, (2) investments and grants for ecosystem partners supporting underrepresented founders, and (3) a Diversity Pledge, whereby all our direct investment portfolio companies commit to improving the recruitment, promotion, and retention of diverse talent.

Outside of PayPal, Mario is also the cofounder of Blueprint Project, a six-week masterclass aimed at supporting the next generation of diverse venture capital investors. The course includes intimate conversations with venture capital luminaries around foundational investment skills and frameworks.

Mario believes there are three key obstacles that are preventing more Latinos from entering venture capital, all of which he believes are attainable with the help and support of the venture capital ecosystem.

1. **Lack of overlapping networks:** Historically, very few Latinos have become venture capitalists or have received venture capital, therefore, we tend to have weaker networks in the ecosystem. Venture capital tends to operate under a "warm introduction" model whereby those who are familiar or have preexisting relationships have greater access to the network. I believe as more Latinos enter venture capital, there is an opportunity and responsibility to "pay it forward" by helping to coach, mentor, and train other aspiring Latino venture capitalists.

2. **Access to information:** Venture capital is a very teachable industry and has historically been an apprenticeship model where seasoned investors help to mentor

and train those rising through the ranks. To lower the barrier of entry for Latinos, there need to be more opportunities where aspiring investors are provided with information on how to build the requisite frameworks and skills to successfully interview and obtain jobs in venture. This point is a key reason he decided to create the Blueprint Project to democratize access to the information that he and many others have built over their careers.

3. **Possibility models:** Since there are very few Latinos in venture capital, it can be difficult to become what you cannot see. There are very few people in the industry we can point to as exemplars of success to model our careers after. Mario believes there is a powerful opportunity with storytelling to shine light on the various pathways to break into venture capital so that aspiring investors can envision their own journey.

His biggest piece of advice for those looking to break into venture capital is to lean into their story. All of us have a unique path to where we are today, and those stories are immensely powerful in showing our grit, determination, and resilience. Mario is a firm believer in measuring someone's success based on their distance traveled, and the best way to highlight your personal journey is to be vulnerable and open about the challenges you have had to overcome. When Mario reflects on the venture capital industry, this can also become a superpower when speaking and empathizing with founders who have also had to withstand great obstacles and challenges to start their companies.

Jorge A. Plasencia
Cofounder, Chairman, and CEO
Republica Havas

Never let the fear of striking out keep you from playing the game.

– Babe Ruth

As cofounder and chairman emeritus, Jorge A. Plasencia sits on the board of Amigos for Kids. Jorge is also on the board of directors of the Friends of the National Museum of the American Latino, the Adrienne Arsht Center for the Performing Arts, and the Miami-Dade County Cultural Affairs Council. Previously, he was chairman of the board of UnidosUS, the nation's largest civil rights and advocacy organization.

Jorge and his brother were both born in the United States, because his parents were exiled from Cuba. He grew up in Miami, Florida. His parents raised them to be grateful to this country and to be humble about everything in life. He never wants to lose that humility. He always reminds himself to take a break, to give back, and to appreciate what has been accomplished.

Since Jorge was a little boy, he has always known he was hardwired to be an entrepreneur. He was the kid on his block with a lemonade stand. As he got older, he realized that getting a proper education was crucial to becoming a successful entrepreneur.

Jorge became a second-generation college graduate and earned a Bachelor of Science with honors from Barry

University. He was also inducted into the Miami Dade College Hall of Fame, and he attended the Advanced Management Education program at Northwestern University, Kellogg School of Management.

The pandemic has made America's digital divide more evident than ever. There is a misconception that the digital divide is more common in rural than urban area, due to the lack of infrastructure to access broadband services. However, the cost of broadband services also plays a big role in who has access.

A lack of internet access can be detrimental to the development of Latino communities. For families with children, a lack of access to the internet inhibits them from accessing the educational tools they need. During the pandemic, many parents struggled to have their children attend school via digital platforms. In today's interconnected world, having access to the internet is a fundamental human right.

With the Latino population in the United States heavily concentrated in some of the country's largest metropolitan areas, including Miami, New York, Los Angeles, and Houston, we must advocate for free and more affordable access to broadband across metropolitan and rural areas.

Jorge's career has been the definition of evolution. Prior to cofounding Republica Havas in 2006, he held various leadership roles in media, sports, and music. At Univision, he played a key role in developing integration and cross-platform opportunities for their television, radio, and digital properties. During his tenure at Estefan Enterprises, he was part of the team that introduced artists such as Shakira to the U.S. market. And as the first director of Hispanic marketing for the Miami Marlins, they won the Hispanic Marketer of the Year award from the Greater Miami Chamber of Commerce – and on the field, the team won its first World Series championship.

Republica is the culmination of these past experiences.

At Republica Havas, they pride themselves on promoting diversity, equity, and inclusion. As an agency, they cater to both the general and multicultural markets. Diversity comes naturally to them.

With over 23 different nationalities represented, it's simply normal for them to embrace many different viewpoints and cultural nuances in the workplace – but they can always do better.

They launched The Greater Good, a DE&I Committee, to propel their efforts toward building connections, acceptance, and support for each of their employees. The initiative focuses on mental health, parental support, youth, community, and career development, and employee retention efforts.

Since great ideas can come from anywhere, they have an open-door policy, meaning that anyone can submit their thoughts and ideas, whether it's a way to strengthen a client pitch or something that can improve their office or organization. They encourage participation, and it's as simple as sending a message through Google Chat.

Today there are 62.3 million Hispanics in the United States, making up 19 percent of the current population. They are frequently making headlines for being key contributors to the economy, labor force, and electorate.

That said, there is still a lot of work to be done regarding representation in corporate America. According to the Hispanic Sentiment Study conducted by We Are All Human, 77 percent of respondents were unaware of recent accomplishments achieved by the Hispanic community across the country. What does that say about how brands are representing this community in the public eye? This problem stems from a lack of representation across leadership levels of government and corporate entities. This lack of representation can often translate into salary disparities, barriers to advancement, and bias at the workplace, to name a few.

The good news is that Jorge believes we have a lot of room to grow and improve diversity in the workforce. Companies and governments need to embrace diversity. They need to hire Hispanics to increase representation across all industries. They need to be prepared to support this workforce, promote Hispanics into leadership roles, and retain talent in order to ensure they are fostering an inclusive environment for Hispanic employees.

For Jorge, keeping an eye on the prize is about opening doors for those who have faced discrimination in the past and to continue advocating for and supporting a more diverse corporate America.

As the world becomes more dependent on digital connectivity, the internet has grown to become a fundamental part of our society and, therefore, a basic human right. Like water and electricity, it has become an essential utility across the United States and the world.

One of the biggest internet misconceptions is that it is a luxury. In reality, the internet is a vital resource – a source of information and a global connective force that can profoundly impact the course of someone's life. The pandemic proved this point even more.

Although America has recently made great strides toward diminishing the digital divide, the FCC estimates that close to 19 million Americans still lack broadband access.

The digital divide is rooted in a lack of financial resources and education. Under-resourced Americans continue to be the group most affected by a lack of broadband. Perpetuating this cycle puts younger generations at a disadvantage in terms of the education, government resources, and opportunities they can access. Jorge does, however, applaud companies, such as Comcast, that are helping to bridge the divide through connectivity programs for the under-resourced.

CONCLUSION

SINCE THE DAWN OF HUMANKIND, we have used technology to augment our capabilities. These external augmentations have caused the directed evolution of humanity. When we first developed fire, we exported digestion from within the body to an external source, which allowed the expansion of food sources and led to agricultural and societal developments that moved humanity forward. With the onset of the new millennium come new challenges to humanity with the exponential rate of technological evolution. These challenges require a new approach that is centered and precise for the Latinx community. Frank and I have sought out leaders throughout the Latinx community who have reached the pinnacle of success within the pillars of industry. Through their stories we have shown that the key to success in this new millennium requires a comprehensive systems approach.

That approach encompasses the DIGITAL approach we have set forth.

We have seen that for the Latinx leaders of today to be prepared to take on the challenges of tomorrow they must be ready to be intentional decision-makers who bring communication, commitment, capacity building, and community that is centrally Latino to high-pressure situations, which will continue to increase with the rate of exponential change in this new digital age. We have seen how Latina and Latino have done this to transform boardrooms across the United States and across industry sectors.

We learned that intelligence is integral for the evolution of the future Latinx leader. This intelligence must be not just external but internal as well. It must encompass not only objective data but emotional intelligence to our fellow humanity and to self-care. This is essential for leaders to maintain servant leadership and not lose the core ethos of their vision and values. It is critical for managing individuals and groups who are bombarded with the ever-growing complexity of life and work balance in this new digital age.

This helps lead into the next stage of the DIGITAL evolution, which is maintaining an inspirational vision that can lead people in this new age. Throughout human history, visionary leaders have always been a part of any revolution. This ability to be a revolutionary leader has now been opened to any and every individual due to the expansion of the internet, social media, and instant communication from any person, anywhere, at any moment. Technology has transported this power from only the pinnacles of power to the fingertips of all in the span of a few decades. This power carries with it a responsibility to DIGITAL leaders to lead wisely and with empathetic intentionality to do well and do good for shareholders, employees, and the world.

The evolution of inclusion is foundational to Latinx leaders and organizations that wish to lead in today's DIGITAL age. We have seen the consequences and disparities that the lack of inclusion has caused throughout history. We have seen how systemic inequalities have led to growing disparities for those who do not conform to the normative majority. As the Latinx community evolves into the majority in the decades to come, we must learn from the mistakes of the past and determine to never repeat them. We know that inclusion has been the driving force of innovation and success for all industries. Our future leaders must embody this ethos as we continue to fight for diversity, equity, and inclusion for all.

Technology will continue to lead the way in this new age of DIGITAL evolution. As technology has evolved, so too have the successful leaders of today. The Latinx leaders of tomorrow must continue to harness emerging technology to transform companies and sectors across the world. But we have to be cognizant that for this to occur we must ensure that the digital divide is defeated. This continues to be a stumbling block to BIPOC communities that must be addressed by a savvy combination of public–private partnerships. Education hinges on access. There is nothing today that cannot be overcome through education, but we must ensure that our future Latinx leaders have the appropriate tools to build that future. The foundation of technology must start early for those skillsets to flourish.

At the core of innovation and entrepreneurship lies abundance, which comes from the arts, media, and entertainment.

We see that for future STEM (science, technology, engineering, and mathematics) leaders, the addition of abundance and the arts to create STEAM is key. This addition is central to our shared humanity and is the cornerstone of the Latino community. By infusing our culture into all that we do, we bring and ensure abundance for all. The arts is the spark of humanity that allows a functional communication tool to turn into the icon we now know as the iPhone. This has been at the root of humanity's greatest thinkers, from Leonardo to Einstein, and must be incorporated for Latinx leaders to lead the future of human-centered innovation.

To whom much is given, much is required. As the Latinx leaders of tomorrow continue to expand their scope and reach, we must remember to use our newfound power to leverage expanded access for those who follow. As *mi abuelo* used to say, "José, make two free clinics for every one that makes you money." We must learn the importance of harnessing leverage to expand innovation within our sectors and throughout our community. In the end, the utilization of this leverage to expand the return on investment for our communities is economical, strategic, and the fuel for the engine of innovation for Latinx leaders.

The DIGITAL evolution of the future Latinx leader is driven by the principles – Decision Making, Intelligence, Game Plan, Inclusion, Technology, Abundance, and Leverage. We have seen how the Latinx leaders of today have used aspects of this design throughout their careers to climb higher, reach further, and continue to shatter glass ceilings throughout industries. The legendary Latinx leaders of today have shown us what it takes to become the titans of tomorrow. Throughout all the lessons of innovation, entre-preneurship, and leadership, one lesson rises above the rest – education. The importance of inspiring our future Latinx leaders must begin with STEAM education, both formal and informal. We must provide inspiration to them at all levels of growth. We must plant the seeds of inspiration that will lead to dreams and stories of their choosing. Inspiration and inno-vation must be nurtured and must be conveyed to the future generations through media education. If they can't see it, they can't be it. We must continue to pursue policies that will eliminate the digital divide that plagues BIPOC communi-ties to ensure that the methods in which STEAM education reaches our communities are not hampered. STEAM educa-tion must be imbued into all aspects of future generations' lives. This is the way to lead the formation of the future DIGITAL Latinx leaders of tomorrow. This is our time to lead the industries of earth today and in the industries in the stars tomorrow – *Ad astra.*

ACKNOWLEDGMENTS

WITH GRATITUDE AND A FULL heart as I write this book, I think about my parents, who have passed away. My mom Hermelinda Carbajal passed in 2019, and my dad Regino Carbajal in 2017. They were married for 54 years, and they truly were my role models. I think of them daily, and I am motivated every day, now more than ever, by the true understanding of their journey and what it took for them as immigrants from Mexico to the United States to make it. I reflect on how they did everything they could for myself and my four siblings.

My parents will always be my true heroes, in my heart and soul.

I would like to thank my wife Molly Carbajal for being the backbone of our family, an amazing wife and an even more incredible mother to our three beautiful and wonderful children, Alia, Myla, and Bria Carbajal, who inspire me every morning to be my best and at the end of each day to reflect on how blessed I am to have three incredible daughters who make me feel complete. I love them more than anything in this world.

I would like to give an amazing thank-you to my mother-in-law, Estela, who has been the most incredibly caring and giving grandmother to my children. Estela is always there for my children.

Thank you to my siblings: Jisela Tafoya, Ray Carbajal, Maria Duenes, and Diana Gutierrez.

My sister Jisela is not only my oldest sister, but also when I was a kid she took me to see my first American mainstream movies, because my parents didn't speak English. My sister Jisela spoiled me; she was like a second mom when my parents had to work two jobs to make ends meet. My brother, Ray Carbajal, and his best friend, Donnie Vercher, who were both like brothers to me. Donnie always had my back in the community where I grew up. Our neighborhood placed an emphasis on respect and one had to stay focused, and Ray and Donnie made sure I stayed focused in school. While growing up my brother, Ray, was my hero!

My sister Maria from a very young age always believed that I would do great in school. From the time she tutored me in the second grade to buying me my first old-school Brother word processor when I was at San José State in the early 1990s, she made sure I stayed on track to graduate.

My sister Diana is closest to my age. When we were growing up we were inseparable, always enjoying time with friends who lived across the street, and we spent many hours at

Eastridge Mall together. I enjoyed visiting my sister Diana at her first job inside the mall, many priceless times.

Thanks to my sisters' spouses: Henry Tafoya, Albert Duenes, and Hugo Gutierrez.

I am grateful all my nieces and nephews, and so proud of all of them.

Thanks to my godparents Vicente and Licha Perez.

I would like to acknowledge all of my childhood friends from Meadow Fair to the East Side Schools, where I grew up. All the friends I played street football and baseball with are part of my most memorable childhood moments.

Thanks to Mark Villarreal and Richard Villarreal, dear friends who are like family.

To Brenda Villalobos, family friend and an incredible nurse.

To Joey Robles, who has always been like a compadre, and from the earlier years as a NSHMBA member to now, thanks to Michael J. Garcia for our great friendship.

Special thanks to my mentors and good friends: Antonio Tijerino, Manny Barbara, Paul Kilkenny, Dick Gonzales, Michael Lopez, Aida Alvarez, Victor Arias, Margarita Quihuis, and Roberto Medrano.

I would like to also thank some folks to whom I spoke early on when I first started writing books: Jesse Wiley; my friend Anna Isabel Espino; Jose Bolanos; and family friends Josef Manuel Liles, Ed Vargas, Luis Alberto Lecanda, Alejandra Chapparo, Frank Rojas, and Felipe Varon.

Also a special thank-you to friends, dear friends who believed in my Silicon Valley Latino Leadership Summit early on: cousins Luis Loe, Imelda Loe, David Sandate, Marcela Sandate, Julie Matsushima, and her husband, Mel Matsushima, who passed in the Spring of 2021; Martin Mares,

Sylvia Kennedy, Mario Vargas, and Raj Chahal; Leonardo Ortiz, Ricky Ortiz, Marco Ramirez, Angelina Ramos, and our family friend Jo Lopez, owner at LUNA Mexican Kitchen; and my family friend and Es Tiempo, LLC Attorney Clay Deanhardt.

Lastly, with gratitude it is an honor to be on the advisory board for Angeles Investors, OppJar, and the Silicon Valley Education Foundation.

—**Frank Carbajal**

To my family, who has sustained me, taught me, nurtured me and loved me – to you I owe it all. A special gracias to my Abuela and my mother, who have been the foundation on which our generations build. We are nothing without you. To my father, thank you for your wit and wisdom. To my son, you will forever be my greatest achievement. *Te amo mucho*.

—**José Morey**

ABOUT THE AUTHORS

Frank Carbajal is founder and president of Es Tiempo, LLC, founder of the Silicon Valley Latino Leadership Summit (SVLLS), and the #365LatinoLeader and the #365LatinaLeader, and coauthor of *Building the Latino Future: Success Stories for the Next Generation.* He sits on the Advocacy Committee for the Silicon Valley Education Foundation and is an Advisory Member for Angeles Investors and Advisory Board Member for OppJar.

Mr. Carbajal holds an MA, with an emphasis in human resources management. He lives with his wife and three daughters in Santa Clara, California.

José Morey is CEO of Ad Astra Media and a 2021 Eisenhower Fellow. He is considered the first intergalactic doctor and is a leader in emerging technology and innovation and sits on the Forbes Technology Council. He is an advisor to MIT SOLVE and IDEAS accelerators, NASA, and the United Nations World Food Program, and has served as a Special Advisor to the White House Office of Science and Technology Policy. He is an AI Ambassador for DeepLearning. AI, and has served as Associate Chief Health Officer for IBM Watson and Chief Engineering Counsel for Hyperloop Transportation Technologies. Dr. Morey holds faculty positions at Singularity University, University of Virginia, and Eastern Virginia Medical School. He is often featured on the MIT Legatum Center for Entrepreneurship, *Forbes*, CNBC, *Nature*, and NASA360. Dr. Morey is passionate about bringing diversity, equity, and inclusion to STEM and believes that science should be as diverse as the world around us. *Ad astra – to the stars!*

INDEX